KLOPP

The Liverpool FC Celebration

KLOPP

The Liverpool FC Celebration

TEN SPEED PRESS

California | New York

CONTENTS

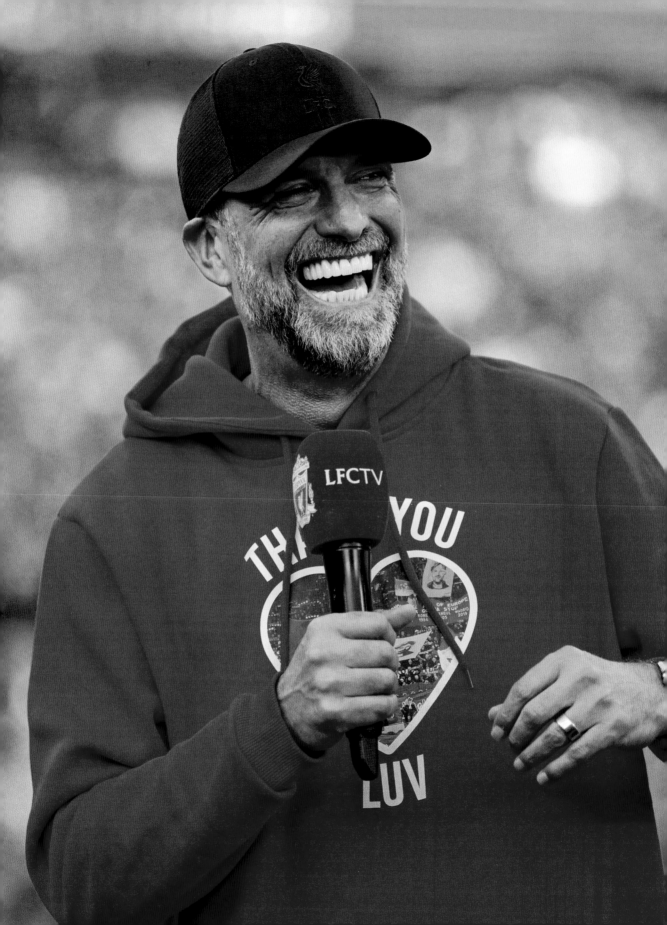

FOREWORD BY JÜRGEN KLOPP

The time I had at Liverpool could not have been more special. There will be those who will say that we could have been more successful and they will be right because the small margins went against us at key moments more often than we would have liked. But in terms of what we did, how we did it and what it meant, I am pretty certain it could not have meant more. I say this not as a boast but as a testament to a period of my life that I would not change. As the song goes, those were the days, my friend.

That Liverpool is an incredible club with unbelievable supporters is not news. I knew this long before I arrived and I definitely was not alone in this knowledge. What I did not know – and it is only with the benefit of experience and hindsight that I can acknowledge this – is just how incredible the club is and just how unbelievable the supporters are. To have shared almost nine years with both was an extraordinary experience and a wonderful privilege. This was the journey of a lifetime and what made it better still was the people I was able to share that journey with.

Central to this, of course, were the players and staff. I have never made any secret of the fact that I have a lifelong love and admiration for footballers with remarkable talent and at Liverpool I was blessed to work alongside so many who affected me in this way. What they achieved and what some of them will go on to achieve is a reflection of the ability they have, the work that they put in on a daily basis and the support that they have had along the way. It is a joint effort involving many different individuals but, ultimately, it is always down to the player to take the most important steps and in this regard I was fortunate to work with so many who were determined to make them.

By doing this, they not only furthered their own careers, they made Liverpool a better, stronger club and they played their part in a story that does not become any less captivating when it is retold. The same goes for the staff that I had with me. This is not just the ones you may know either. It is the people at front of house and the workers behind the scenes. It is everyone who I shared this journey with, too many to mention but also far, far too important not to be acknowledged. It is also the owners who created the conditions that allowed such a special period to happen.

There is only one word to describe the contribution that they all made – immense. Whatever we did, we did together. It was never one person, it was always a group acting together in the best interests of Liverpool FC. Without this

approach I know the outcomes we had would have been impossible. I could not respect or appreciate them more. This is why I am so pleased that players and colleagues have provided some of the lead voices for this project. It is their story, it is our story and it is also your story. It is ours to tell, ours to enjoy, ours to share, and we should cherish it for these reasons.

The different perspectives are of huge interest to me, just as I am sure they will be to anyone who reads this book. I have my own and shared them publicly during my nine years as manager but I was always aware that others are available and that there would not always be alignment. That is the beauty of football – we are all allowed to have views and opinions and it is absolutely allowed that we put them in whichever order and whichever context we like. These players and colleagues may not realise it at the time because they are – how shall I put this? – too busy with other things but as well as being part of history, they are also first-hand witnesses to history so it makes a lot of sense that their recollections are given this kind of platform.

In doing so, I hope we are able to add another dimension to what is already known. As someone who has always read and enjoyed stories from football's past and present and been enchanted by the photographs that capture moments in time, I have been excited to see the outcome and I hope you are too. Again, though, I have to stress that the story belongs not to me but to all of us who were fortunate to be involved in it in any way. From the supporter in the stands to the player on the pitch, from the worker in the ticket office to the owner in the boardroom, and from the cleaner at the training ground to the ground staff at the stadium, we all get to own it between us.

This is how I understand Liverpool and it is also how I understand life. Someone might have to be at the forefront because that is what the world demands but at most they are only ever first among equals. Pushing a club of LFC's size in the right direction takes a lot of bodies and just as many minds. My honour was being given the opportunity to play my part but I always knew that whatever we achieved was only made possible by the many, many brilliant people who wanted to push in the same direction. Together, we might not have always been able to get to our destination but we were always able to share an unforgettable journey while enjoying some success and incredible moments along the way.

Some journeys live forever and this is definitely one of them.

You'll Never Walk Alone.
Jürgen

INTRODUCTION

October 2015 to May 2024 was an amazing time to be a Liverpool supporter. A period that is right up there with the greatest in this club's history.

The Jürgen Klopp era was a roller-coaster ride of emotions. Eight and a half years of unbelievable highs and excruciating lows. Tears of joy and tears of sadness. Celebrations and commiserations. Yet the good times far outweighed the bad.

Jürgen's arrival from Borussia Dortmund generated a huge buzz of excitement and plenty of hope amongst a success-starved fanbase, but not even the most optimistic of Liverpudlians could have foreseen the glory he would bring.

From heavy metal football and mentality monsters to journey hunters and history makers. Not only did Jürgen fully succeed in turning doubters into believers, he created memories that will last a lifetime and made everyone's wildest dreams come true.

This adopted Scouser from the Black Forest in Germany reunited the club, restored pride and re-established the team as an all-conquering force that swept across football pitches at home and abroad like a powerful tornado, gathering up silverware in its wake. He took Liverpool back to the top level and kept them there, consistently challenging for the game's major honours and completely revolutionising the way we see football at Anfield.

This book traces the most pivotal and memorable moments of his tenure, including the countless trips across the continent, the days out at Wembley and the moments when we never gave up. It was difficult to know just where to begin; there were so many stories, we were spoilt for choice. So, we turned to those who know him best to gain added insight.

From some of the key figures who worked alongside him within the club through some of Liverpool's heroes who played under him, to some of his most high-profile competitors, each provide their own personal view as to the special qualities Jürgen possessed.

Mike Gordon explains what it was about Jürgen that made him the perfect fit for Liverpool. James Milner talks about how Jürgen set about transforming the club's fortunes. Mo Salah and Virgil van Dijk outline how Jürgen convinced them to sign for him. Jordan Henderson reveals how Jürgen's team talk inspired their legendary comeback against Barcelona in 2019. Mauricio Pochettino describes how it felt to face Jürgen's team as they became Champions of Europe for a sixth time. Roberto Firmino speaks about how Jürgen supported his players into becoming champions of the world for the first time. Sir Alex Ferguson recalls

the celebratory call he received from Jürgen Klopp after they became champions of England and ended the 30-year wait. And Pep Lijnders tells us what it was like to work so closely with Jürgen on a daily basis. These are just a few examples of the recollections you will find in a book that places you right in the heart of Jürgen's incredible Liverpool journey.

With a bit more luck here and there, a few more trophies may have been delivered, but apart from the odd result, there isn't much we would change about a managerial reign that has had everyone captivated from day one.

All Jürgen ever wanted was the best for Liverpool Football Club and its supporters. He was a manager in tune with the fanbase and they adored him on a scale not witnessed at Anfield since the days of Bill Shankly. Comparisons with the late, great Scotsman are genuine. To the modern generation of Liverpudlians Jürgen was, is and always will be their version of Shankly.

Jürgen walked in the footsteps of so many legendary managers at Anfield and walks away as a legend himself. A true King of the Kop who won almost everything,

leaving Liverpool as the only manager to lift trophies in six different competitions.

Despite his success, the self-proclaimed 'Normal One' remained true to his roots and fully embraced life in this city. As an adopted Scouser he understood what the people were about, was sympathetic to local causes and would go out of his way to help whenever and wherever he could. Jürgen loved Liverpool and Liverpool loved him. The connection we felt was far from normal. It was special.

His list of endearing qualities is endless. He was humble, he was honest and his passion shone through at every opportunity. The fist pumps, the bear hugs and the huge beaming smile were authentic. What you saw with Jürgen is what you got.

The glasses, the beard and the baseball cap will forever remain iconic symbols of a remarkable time in our lives. Not to mention, of course, the silverware.

Jürgen Klopp will be sorely missed but he'll never be forgotten. This book is a celebration of his story at Liverpool, one we will never tire of telling.

Above:
One of the most important appointments ever made by the club, Jürgen's popularity knew no bounds.

THE NORMAL ONE

2015–16

"Jürgen and I hit it off during our very first phone conversation. It was pretty clear to me by the time I hung up that he was the right person. We then arranged a meeting in New York City, had a lengthy discussion late one night and another the following day, and it was even more apparent that Jürgen was the perfect choice. With eight trophies in nine years, he helped the club reach new heights in a place renowned for its historic achievements. His impact was not only defined by incredible leadership of our team, but by his genuine compassion and humanity off the pitch. He has been instrumental in helping us build something extraordinary and durable in Liverpool for which he will always have our heartfelt gratitude and lasting friendship."

MIKE GORDON PRESIDENT,
FENWAY SPORTS GROUP

WELCOME TO ANFIELD

Jürgen's First Press Conference

Anfield, Friday 9 October 2015… The start of a new chapter in the illustrious history of Liverpool Football Club.

For the past six days only one story had dominated the football headlines and it centred around the managerial position here.

The previous evening, following days of speculation in the aftermath of Brendan Rodgers being relieved of his duties, it was confirmed on the club's official website that stepping into the void would be 48-year-old German Jürgen Norbert Klopp.

After jetting into John Lennon Airport on a private plane from Dortmund, one that was tracked on the internet by over 35,000 people, Klopp had put pen to paper on the deal in the city's Hope Street Hotel, observed by club chairman Tom Werner and chief executive officer Ian Ayre.

The former Mainz 05 and Borussia Dortmund boss had long been the front-runner to take the reins, so while the announcement came as no big surprise, the excitement and interest it sparked were unprecedented.

For the red half of Merseyside, and the many millions of Liverpool supporters further afield, it felt like Christmas had come two months early. From what they had already seen and knew of him, Klopp seemed like the most natural fit for the job

Above: Jürgen speaks to the media at his unveiling press conference.

and was the manager their hearts had been set on ever since the previous manager had departed.

More importantly, he also ticked all the boxes on checklists of those tasked with finding the right man to wake the sleeping giant that was Liverpool FC.

Despite having come agonisingly close to pulling off a remarkable Premier League title triumph just 18 months before, dark clouds had been gathering once again over this famous old stadium.

The one-time undisputed Kings of English and European football had been living in the shadows for far too long, a succession of would-be messiahs having come and gone after failing to re-establish the Reds as the mighty all-conquering force they once were.

At a club of Liverpool's stature, expectations are high, and following a poor start to the 2015/16 season, which left the team languishing tenth in the Premier League table, Rodgers became the latest managerial casualty.

Could Klopp be the man to finally buck this trend, restore pride and lead the club back to where every supporter believed they rightfully belonged?

His achievements in Dortmund, where he succeeded in toppling the perennial Bundesliga giants Bayern Munich, certainly vindicated the renewed air of optimism that was suddenly swirling around Anfield. Smiles were back on Liverpudlian faces and fans now gathered in huge numbers outside the Shankly Gates, waiting with bated breath to hear how he planned to set about reviving former glories.

Although club football was in the midst of an international break, the world's media had descended on L4 for Jürgen's official unveiling. This was the most eagerly anticipated press conference for years and deep in the bowels of what is now the Sir Kenny Dalglish Stand, journalists crammed into the 'Reds Lounge', where space was at a premium.

As the clock ticked towards the scheduled start time, the buzz of anticipation grew. Cameramen jostled for the best vantage point, while the scribes made last-minute adjustments to their list of pre-planned questions. Speculative chatter filled the room until a hushed silence swept over it as, on cue, the main man entered the arena.

Dressed smart-casual in a dark shirt and blazer, upturned jeans and Chelsea boots, Klopp immediately exuded an air of cool confidence. Refreshed by a four-month hiatus following those seven years of intense 'heavy metal gegenpressing' in the Ruhr Valley, he appeared completely relaxed and happily flashed his trademark beaming smile at the cameras that strove to capture his every move.

As the club's Head of Press Matt McCann went through the preliminaries, Klopp took his seat at the top table alongside Ian Ayre, before Peter McDowall, Anfield's pitch-side announcer and presenter for the club's in-house television channel LFCTV, opened proceedings.

Opposite:
Getting familiar with his new surroundings, Jürgen touches the famous 'This Is Anfield' sign.

"Good morning, Jürgen. Welcome to Liverpool Football Club. What attracted you to this challenge? How do you feel?" Although he needn't have, Klopp firstly apologised for his English then set off on what was an unplanned but perfectly delivered charm offensive.

"It's the biggest honour to be at one of the biggest clubs in this world," he boldly proclaimed. "I feel really proud. I'm looking forward to the intensity of football and how the people live football in Liverpool. It's a special club. I'm not a dreamer but I'm a football romantic. I love the stories and Anfield is one of the best places in the football world."

The new boss had hit the right notes straight from the off and that was just the start. Anyone who had harboured doubts about his credentials for the job – and there weren't many – had been won over already, his infectious and bubbly persona impressing even the most hardened of hacks.

Laughing and joking throughout the 26-minute briefing, Klopp reiterated he was very much a 'lucky guy' to be the new Liverpool manager but, when required, also displayed a more serious side to his nature. He spoke openly and honestly about his life and career to date, the task he now faced and the legends whose footsteps he was following in.

"I don't compare myself with these geniuses within the history of Liverpool," he added. "None of these managers said they wanted to be a legend when they arrived. This is a great club because of many good decisions in the past. Now we have to work in the present. I don't live in the past. History is only the base for us. You cannot carry it in your backpack every day. I want to see the first steps next week, but we must not always compare. Being 100% in the moment is the only possibility to get better in the future."

When quizzed on what supporters could expect to see from his team, the new man at the helm promised 'full-throttle football' and confidently predicted a trophy within four years, but stressed the need for patience and belief in the project.

"It is a good moment to reset, that's for sure, but it's important that we play our own game, that the players feel the confidence and trust of the people. They have to think they can reach the expectations of everyone. We must change from doubters to believers. It's a very important thing. In a special Liverpool way, we can be successful.

"When I left Dortmund I said, 'It's not important what people say when you come in; it's what they think when you leave.' Now I say: Please give us time to work, please be patient. Today could be a very special day."

It was, however, what he said midway through this inaugural Anfield press conference that would come to define his arrival as Liverpool manager, a quote delivered with unintentional innocence but one that has since passed into Kop folklore and would even inspire a new range of official club merchandise.

Above: The new boss takes a look around Anfield's home team dressing room.

It stemmed from a question about his popularity and how he would describe himself in relation to then Chelsea manager Jose Mourinho's famous self-declaration that he was the 'special one'. After listening intently to what the journalist had to say, Klopp shook his head and laughed.

"I don't want to describe myself. Does anyone in this room think I can do wonder(s)? No. So let me work," was his initial response, before he continued, "I am not going to call myself anything. I am a totally normal guy. I come from the Black Forest. My mother may be sitting in front of the television watching this press conference at home and understood no word until now … but she'll be very proud. I am the normal one. If you are going to call me anything, maybe this."

Howls of laughter filled the room. To the assembled press pack this was pure gold-dust and, amid a litany of priceless soundbites, the stand-out quote that would spread like wildfire around the globe, splashed across headlines on the internet, television and newspapers.

The 'normal one' had indeed arrived and it was a day that is now firmly etched in the annals of Liverpool history. Like the late great former Liverpool manager Bill Shankly 56 years before, Jürgen Klopp had breezed into Anfield like a welcome breath of fresh air and set Liverpudlian pulses racing. The Shankly comparisons wouldn't end there and over the course of the next eight and a half years that breeze would be whipped up into a whirlwind.

A NEW DAWN

Tottenham Hotspur v Liverpool | Premier League, 17 October 2015

White Hart Lane was the venue for Jürgen Klopp's first game as Liverpool manager and it was James Milner who had the honour of captaining the team on this historic occasion.

A summer signing from Manchester City, with whom he won two Premier League titles, the experienced Milner had recently been appointed vice-captain by Brendan Rodgers but had stepped up to wear the armband in the absence of the injured Jordan Henderson.

Nine days had passed since Klopp's appointment but the hype surrounding it had only intensified. All eyes, plus the live television cameras, were focused on how his team would fare with him in charge for the first time.

The side Milner led out that day showed just two changes to the one that started Liverpool's last game and the first selection headache of Klopp's reign centred on who would lead the attack. With Danny Ings having suffered a season-ending knee injury earlier in the week, fellow forwards Christian Benteke and Roberto Firmino sidelined, and Daniel Sturridge then being ruled out on the morning of the match, it meant a full league debut for Divock Origi.

Yet Klopp was itching to get started. When interviewed just prior to kick-off, he spoke about feeling a sense of excitement and pressure but also opportunity. Coming up against a Spurs side that had not lost since the opening day of the season, though, was always going to be tough.

Below left:
James Milner setting the tempo during Jürgen's first game in charge.

Below right:
Alberto Moreno embracing the new manager's full-throttle approach.

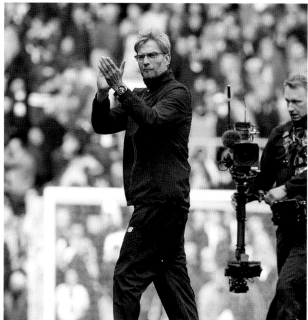

The subsequent goalless draw may have been deemed an anti-climax by some, but not by the new boss. "Nil-nil is not my dream result but it is okay. I am happy because I saw many good things in my team today. We were pressing and were very aggressive. We will get stronger, but after working with the players for three days, I am completely satisfied."

Although Origi headed against the bar early on, goalscoring opportunities for Liverpool were few and far between, and it was widely viewed as a point gained rather than two lost. The fact that goalkeeper Simon Mignolet was many pundits' choice as man-of-the-match shows just what direction the balance of play largely swung, but the red shirts dug deep when under pressure and ran their hearts out for the cause. Klopp had placed a big emphasis on improving the energy levels of his players and they managed to cover more ground (116km) than in any other game so far that season.

On the touchline, Klopp's actions mirrored the efforts of his players. He hardly stood still throughout the entire 90 minutes, a trait that would soon become commonplace whenever Liverpool played.

The galvanising effect of his appointment was already plain to see and that extended to the mood among the fanbase. The 3,000 Liverpudlians who had made the long journey south for this midday kick-off sang nonstop and waved German tricolours in his honour, while, in response to a plea he had made in his first press conference, another banner simply read 'We Believe'.

At the final whistle, Klopp came onto the pitch to embrace his players and salute those fans. A new era was officially underway.

Above left:
The travelling Reds show their support for the new boss.

Above right:
A new era is underway and the cameras are tracking Jürgen's every move.

Next page:
James Milner and Danny Rose in the heat of battle at White Hart Lane.

"From his first day here, it was immediately clear what he wanted. It was all heavy metal football at one thousand miles per hour and the tempo against Spurs was ludicrously high, totally different to what we had been used to. Everyone was struggling to keep up with the pace of the game, but he was constantly screaming encouragement from the touchline, and that's how it would be from that point forward. 'We need to create our own history,' he said, and this was us setting out to achieve that. He had a vision, and together we would go on some journey. It had ups and downs but so many special moments. What you saw with Jürgen is what you got, there was no other side to him. From his famous hugs to how he expertly judged narratives around games, it was great playing for a manager like him."

JAMES MILNER

LIFT OFF

Chelsea v Liverpool | Premier League, 31 October 2015

It was billed as 'The Special One' versus 'The Normal One'. The old master against the new pretender. Jose Mourinho and Jürgen Klopp going head to head in the Premier League for the first time.

In reality, if it hadn't been for the managers, this was nothing more than a meeting between two relatively mediocre sides, neither of whom were expected to challenge for the title. But these two clubs and the respective men in charge were at different ends of the scale and heading in opposite directions. There lay the intrigue.

Klopp was only three weeks into the job, with just two Premier League games under his belt, whereas Mourinho was a three-time Premier League champion and the most successful manager of his generation. Yet, following a dismal start to the campaign, he was now teetering towards the brink at Stamford Bridge.

It was still far too early to judge Klopp's impact at Liverpool. The uplift in the mood around the club was clear, but it was fair to say that it hadn't been the best of starts when it came to the results: his first four games had yielded three draws and a win, that solitary victory coming against Bournemouth in the League Cup.

When Ramires opened the scoring for Chelsea after just four minutes, another frustrating afternoon seemingly lay in store. As the half wore on, though, Liverpool got a foothold in the game. As half-time approached, they were the more threatening side.

The hosts were defending desperately and hanging on for the half-time whistle. Mourinho was already waiting at the edge of the tunnel when Philippe Coutinho deservedly equalised.

The game remained in the balance for much of the second half. At times tempers became frayed, until an inspired Klopp substitution helped swing the pendulum back in Liverpool's favour.

Sensing the game was opening up, the manager gambled. For the first time since taking charge, the change he made was, positionally, not like-for-like. Striker Christian Benteke was sent on in place of the more defensive James Milner and immediately began to make his imposing presence felt. In the 74th minute his aerial strength saw him nod the ball into the path of Coutinho, who doubled his tally with a shot that deflected into the net.

Eight minutes from time, Benteke sealed victory by drilling the ball home after being ably assisted by fellow substitute Jordon Ibe.

It capped an excellent Liverpool performance, comfortably the best yet under Klopp. "Sometimes you have to work really, really hard to make football look easy. That is what we did today," said the manager afterwards.

For Mourinho, so often the scourge of Liverpool in the past, it had been a Halloween horror show. The end was nigh for him; six weeks later he was dismissed.

After a couple of false starts, this was the day that Jürgen Klopp really announced himself to the Premier League. Chelsea may not have been the force they were in 2014/2015, but this was a statement win for Liverpool against the reigning champions, Klopp's first away from Anfield and his first in the Premier League.

"I was aware of Jürgen's achievements at Borussia Dortmund and Mainz, so we knew a good manager was coming to the club. He's obviously a big character, who was capable of working with the players, to get them ready for games and to keep them motivated, and he made a difference straight away. He was very good tactically and it was clear that he's a winner. He showed it on a daily basis in training and when it comes to a matchday, you could see it in his emotion on the touchline. Everything just came together – him, the players, the fans – and the result at Chelsea was an early sign of what lay in store. Unfortunately, for me, I was only there at the beginning but as a fan I'm happy that we brought him to the club because the trophies eventually came and that's what everyone at Liverpool craved."

MARTIN SKRTEL

COMMUNION WITH THE KOP

Liverpool v West Bromwich Albion | Premier League, 13 December 2015

The root of this now seminal moment can be traced back to events towards the end of the home game with Crystal Palace a month earlier.

On 8 November 2015, with Liverpool trailing 2-1 and the action petering out, sighs of disappointment rang around Anfield. Jürgen Klopp looked for support from the fans behind him in the Main Stand but was shocked to see them leaving early. He wasn't shy in making his feelings known.

It was his first real taste of defeat as Liverpool manager and he admitted afterwards, "I felt pretty alone at that moment."

Liverpool's subsequent four-game winning streak, which included a stunning 4-1 demolition of Manchester City at the Etihad, did much to lift spirits. Yet, these early months of Klopp's Liverpool tenure remained plagued by inconsistency.

Below:
Jordan Henderson celebrates with Adam Lallana after opening the scoring v West Brom.

In December, the team welcomed West Brom to Anfield on the back of two uninspiring away results: a defeat to Newcastle and a goalless draw with FC Sion in the Europa League.

When captain Jordan Henderson, now back fit after injury, put Liverpool ahead in the 21st minute, fans hoped it would signal a return to form once again, only for West Brom to hit back with two goals either side of half-time.

Grumblings of discontent from up in the stands were threatening to surface once more, while down on the pitch tensions were running high. Klopp himself even became embroiled in a touchline altercation with his opposite number Tony Pulis.

With his team hurtling towards a second successive league defeat, Klopp raised his arms, urging the crowd to turn up the volume. This time, everyone responded. No-one left early and the backing was vociferous.

Liverpool could still not conjure up an equaliser. The onslaught towards the Albion goal continued as the game entered injury time and eventually, in the 96th minute, they got their reward. Substitute Divock Origi's speculative shot somehow, from a distance, via a deflection, found its way into the back of the net.

Below:
Super-sub Divock Origi, who rescued a point for the Reds with a late equaliser.

"When Klopp came I found my role in central midfield and that was the breakthrough for me. At first, he was very challenging. If you didn't get to the second ball, he would scream, and the next time, you made sure that you got there double-quick. I learned that you can't do anything without hard work. Everyone needs to run, he would say. Those years were extremely important for my personal and professional development. He changed many things at the club and recognised the importance of the fans. After drawing at home with West Brom he made us all stand together in front of the Kop and salute them. It was a special moment that showed just what a unique manager he is and it meant a lot to him. He went on to build a superb team, and I will always be grateful for the help he gave me."

EMRE CAN

The manic scenes of celebration were way beyond what you would expect for salvaging a point from a home game with West Brom. Klopp could not contain his delight or his emotions. To him, this meant much more. It was proof of what can be achieved with the power of the crowd fully behind the team. At the end of the match, he famously got all the players together and took them to the Kop, where they stood in unison, arms interlinked, to salute the fans who had helped get them over the line.

"I know it's only one point but it felt like three," he said. "This moment was an explosion, it's the best I've felt since I've been here. Sometimes a point deserved in the right way is more important. I really enjoyed this game. I enjoyed the atmosphere with my whole body."

Those looking in from the outside may have mocked, but Klopp had not only reconnected the unique bond that has always existed between the Liverpool team and its supporters, he had strengthened it.

Above:
German mid-fielder Emre Can in action against West Brom at Anfield.

Next page:
Jürgen and his players show their appreciation to supporters on the Kop.

CHAOS & COMEDY AT CARROW ROAD

Norwich City v Liverpool | Premier League, 23 January 2016

While talent and natural ability are key components in the construction of any successful football team, the less glamorous attributes of incessant hard work and an insatiable will-to-win can never be overestimated. These were the foundations on which Jürgen Klopp set out to build his Anfield empire.

As 2015 rolled into 2016, Klopp's assessment of the job he'd done so far would have been mixed. He had instilled a renewed spirit of togetherness throughout the squad, who had won more than they had lost, but results remained unpredictable. In late December, Liverpool had beaten soon-to-be league champions Leicester, then almost suffered a humiliating FA Cup exit against League Two Exeter City, albeit with a heavily rotated side.

Anyone searching for clues as to the true level of Klopp's Liverpool would have again been left scratching their heads on this crazy goal-laden afternoon in East Anglia.

Below: Roberto Firmino, scorer of two goals for the Reds at Carrow Road.

When Roberto Firmino opened the scoring in the 18th minute, there was no indication of the madness that lay ahead, but alarm bells started to ring after haphazard defending saw that early advantage suddenly tossed away.

The root of the problem was Liverpool's inability to successfully defend set-pieces. In three of their most recent games this had proved costly. Over 40% of all the league goals they had conceded that season had originated from such situations and they held the unwanted record of having conceded the most goals from corners.

"It's like a self-fulfilling prophecy," said Klopp. "Everybody's talking about it, we're thinking about it. It's not that difficult. We know how to defend but we have to do it."

By the 54th minute, the game had completely turned on its head, with Norwich racing into a 3-1 lead. Since 1992, Liverpool had only twice before overturned a two-goal deficit in the league to clinch victory and the prospect of them even salvaging a point was now looking slim.

It's at moments like these that real character needs to be shown and fortunately Klopp's team had this in abundance. The manager refused to believe his team were beaten and this was transmitted onto the pitch. While others may have slumped back to the bench, the Reds boss continued to pace frantically up and down the touchline, gesticulating wildly and roaring words of encouragement towards his players. An unlikely comeback ensued as Jordan Henderson, Firmino (again) and James Milner all scored to flip the score back in Liverpool's favour.

Job done? Not quite. The Canaries sang once more and, to Klopp's utter despair, drew level in the second minute of stoppage time. For most managers this would

Below:
Adam Lallana fires home his dramatic late winner in the nine-goal thriller v Norwich.

have been the signal to sit back and accept a point, but there was one final act still to be performed.

With barely seconds remaining, one last hopeful punt into the Norwich box eventually fell perfectly for Adam Lallana, who smashed home a left-footed volley to snatch the win. It was barely believable. The goalscorer whipped off his shirt in celebration and ran towards the bench. A sprinting Klopp was already on his way to meet him. Amid the joyous melee that followed, the manager comically lost his glasses. "I have a second pair but I can't find them. It's really difficult looking for glasses without glasses," he joked afterwards.

While the manic heat-of-the-moment celebrations seemed more akin to a cup final victory, Klopp knew only too well that Lallana's strike had, in reality, only served to paper over the cracks of a project that was very much still a work in progress. It was a performance that highlighted the best and worst of this Liverpool side. "That's how life is," he later mused, "solve one problem and you have another."

"I remember being so excited that Jürgen was going to be our manager. He called himself the 'normal one' but had far too much charisma to be that. There was a heavy weight of expectation at Liverpool, but he took the pressure off us all when he arrived. He just knew how to handle being a Liverpool manager and what that badge meant. This moment has since become pretty iconic, and it came during the early days of his reign. It provoked crazy celebrations, which led to Jürgen's glasses being broken but, thankfully, he never held it against me! He later brought success back to the club, and I just feel lucky to have been part of that. Everything we achieved was down to him, his genius and the aura that surrounded him. No normal manager could have done what he did, and his legacy will be there forever."

ADAM LALLANA

WEMBLEY WOE

Liverpool v Manchester City | League Cup Final, 28 February 2016

Not many managers lead their team to a cup final at Wembley within just four months of being in the job. Jürgen Klopp did.

Following the nine-goal thriller at Norwich, inconsistency continued to plague the Reds, but a six-game winless run was emphatically brought an end with a 6-0 away win at Aston Villa, and progress to the last 16 of the Europa League had been secured courtesy of a two-legged victory over Augsburg.

A first Wembley appearance as Liverpool boss held no fears for Klopp. He had been here before with Borussia Dortmund in 2013, but the memories of that night, a 2-1 Champions League Final defeat to Bundesliga rivals Bayern Munich, remained raw. It was an experience he didn't want to endure again.

In reaching this final, Klopp had brought the feel-good factor back for Liverpool supporters, who he had fully won over with his passion and management style. Although results were still not always to their liking, the direction in which they were being taken was clear.

The much-maligned League Cup held mostly happy memories for Liverpool. They had lifted it a record eight times and, as Bill Shanky once famously said,

Below: Lucas Leiva and David Silva compete for the ball at Wembley.

"Jürgen arriving gave everyone a massive boost and working for someone with his track record was really exciting. Within a few months we reached the League Cup Final and it had always been my dream to play for Liverpool at Wembley. A few hours before kick-off he told me I'd be starting. That was such a special moment. Unfortunately, we couldn't win the game but, I remember afterwards, he remained so positive. You could tell good things were going to happen with him here. He was also a very open guy. I went to see him one day because I wasn't happy about not being in the team and he said, 'Lucas, I can tell you what I think, but it might not be what you want to hear.' I fully respected him for that, and we always had a great relationship. He was a great manager for me."

LUCAS LEIVA

winning trophies is what this club exists for. The status of the competition didn't matter.

Klopp was of a similar mindset and knew the benefits that delivering silverware so early into his reign would bring. But protocol dictated that he had to change from his usual matchday attire of tracksuit and baseball cap into a suit. It didn't look right and proved to be a bad omen.

Liverpool fell behind to a Fernando goal just after half-time but, with seven minutes left, Philippe Coutinho had Klopp punching the air with joy after he equalised to send the game into extra time. There were no further goals and so it was the lottery of a penalty shoot-out that would determine the winners.

Liverpool had defeated Carlisle United in the third round of the competition, a month before Klopp's arrival, and Stoke City in the semi-final in the same way. Unfortunately, though, they had used up their good fortune. Beneath the Wembley arch it proved to be a case of third time unlucky.

Liverpool held the early advantage but Lucas Leiva, Coutinho and Adam Lallana subsequently failed to convert, and the cup went to City. It was the first time Liverpool had lost a cup final on penalties.

Defeat was naturally disappointing, but Klopp vowed that his team would use it to their advantage. "We feel down but now we have to stand up," he said. "Only silly idiots stay on the floor and wait for the next defeat. We will strike back. We will go on and we will get better. We have to work really hard, carry on and there is light at the end of the tunnel. This is important."

The response was instant. When the two teams met again in the league just four nights later, there may have been no trophy at stake, but Liverpool quickly got the Wembley blues out of their system – beating them 3-0. Klopp was right, there was no keeping this team down for long.

Opposite:
Jürgen lines up with his players ahead of his first cup final as Liverpool manager.

Above left:
James Milner can't hide his disappointment as the Reds lose on penalties.

Above right:
Skipper Jordan Henderson attempts to console Phil Coutinho as a dejected Adam Lallana looks on.

RING OF FIRE

Manchester United v Liverpool | Europa League round of 16 2nd leg, 17 March 2016

Liverpool and Manchester United. The two most successful clubs in English football, both with a proud pedigree on the continent. Yet strangely, until 2015/2016 these fierce rivals had never been paired together in European competition.

The game promised to be the kind of high-octane occasion that Jürgen Klopp relished. After years of going toe to toe with Bayern Munich as Borussia Dortmund manager, he was well equipped for the red-hot battle that was England's version of 'Der Klassiker'.

The interest of those who had turned their noses up at the Europa League earlier in the campaign was suddenly piqued. Klopp labelled it "the mother of all games".

Had things played out differently, he could well have been stood on that touchline brandishing a red devil on his chest. It's no secret that before Liverpool appointed him, Manchester United had actively shown an interest in making Klopp their manager. Talks took place but he politely declined their advances and opted to remain at Dortmund, and United's loss was ultimately to be Liverpool's gain. Rejected by the German, it was Dutchman Louis van Gaal who the Old Trafford hierarchy eventually settled on.

Although Van Gaal had got the better of Klopp in the league meeting two months earlier, this Europa League tie provided an early opportunity for revenge. In the first leg at Anfield, Klopp did just that, masterminding a dominant 2-0 Liverpool success on an electric night.

In the return leg a week later, the onus was on United, but Klopp outwitted Van Gaal again.

The Liverpool fans, armed with an array of homemade flags and a vast repertoire of songs in honour of their club's rich history of European success, were in the mood for a party, and not even Anthony Martial's 32nd-minute penalty could dampen their spirits on a St Patrick's night to remember.

The decisive moment arrived on the stroke of half-time, via the twinkle-toed Philippe Coutinho. Allowed too much space, he glided towards goal down the right flank, jinked his way inside the penalty area then delicately dinked the ball past David de Gea from a tight angle. According to Klopp it was the "perfect goal" and "a genius moment".

Liverpool's number ten then coolly jogged past a stunned Stretford End as the travelling Liverpudlians, tucked away in their own little enclave of Old Trafford, lit up the Manchester sky with a celebratory light show.

For the shattered hosts there was no way back and Van Gaal's days were numbered, while Klopp had got his tactics spot on once again. "We deserve to be in the next round, there is no doubt about that. I'm pretty proud of the boys."

It had been five years since United had surpassed Liverpool's once record-breaking haul of English league titles, but it still rankled with them that they remained in the shadows when it came to European success. This defeat rubbed further salt into those wounds.

The Liver Bird was not yet fully back on its perch, but this was further proof that, under Klopp, it was clearly on the right flight path.

Above: Liverpool line up at Old Trafford, ready to defend their 2-0 first-leg advantage.

Next page: Daniel Sturridge, scorer of Liverpool's opening goal in the first leg against Manchester United.

"When Klopp came in everyone bought into his ideas and the project. Working with him was intense. It was rock and roll football, one hundred miles per hour. He took things to a whole new level of intensity, and we were challenging right away, especially in the Europa League. Going to Old Trafford with a 2-0 lead from the first leg was massive. We were confident, of course, but the gaffer also ensured we were mentally prepared to complete the job, which we did. It was a great night and Jürgen was a great manager, different to all the others. I didn't play under him as much as I would have liked but we always had a very good relationship. For what he went on to achieve at Liverpool and for the relationship we still have today, I have nothing but love and respect for the man."

DANIEL STURRIDGE

FRIENDS REUNITED

Liverpool v Borussia Dortmund | Europa League quarter-final 2nd leg, 14 April 2016

At Anfield, nothing evokes dewy-eyed nostalgia more than a trip down the memory lane of thrilling European nights, the likes of which are carved deep into the fabric of this club.

There is a long list of famous continental conquests on home soil that will forever be lauded but in 2016, even the most recent of those unforgettable nights were in danger of becoming a fast-fading memory.

When that happens and there's nothing new to get excited about, thoughts naturally turn to 'how good it was before'. Klopp knew he needed to create new memories. He'd warned when he took charge at the club that the weight of history could sometimes be too big a burden to carry and he wanted new stories to be written.

He wouldn't have believed the opportunity to do so would come just six months into his reign. Especially as the Liverpool team he had inherited were only competing in the Europa League, the perceived second-rate European competition. But after seeing off arch-rivals Manchester United in the previous round, the appetite of the manager, players and supporters had been whetted.

When the quarter-final draw threw up the most intriguing of encounters, they were salivating. Liverpool versus Borussia Dortmund. The Klopp derby, his new love against his previous love, or, as some dubbed it 'El Kloppico'. It was the undoubted tie of the round, a match-up between two former European Cup winners that not only would have graced the final itself but the Champions League too.

Interest in the tie was understandably immense and over 65,000 were at the Westfalenstadion to witness Klopp's emotional return. Although Dortmund were deemed favourites, the first leg proved to be a satisfactory night for Liverpool, who took the lead through Divock Origi in the first half. Although Mats Hummels later equalised, they held on for a valuable 1-1 draw, leaving it tantalisingly poised ahead of the second leg at Anfield the following week.

It had the potential to be a classic and it didn't disappoint. An electric atmosphere was always guaranteed, but this exceeded expectations, even by Liverpool standards.

A stirring and emotional rendition of 'You'll Never Walk Alone', the much-loved anthem of both clubs, was the perfect pre-cursor to a night of raw passion, of flags and flares, scarves and more songs, when the atmosphere touched, if not bettered, the heights of some previous great European nights at Anfield. A kaleidoscope of

"We never lost belief. The manager said to us at half-time, 'Just remember 2005, when Liverpool were 3-0 down against AC Milan in the Champions League Final.' He reminded us that anything is possible and it was. At two down we had stopped playing and heads were down but he gave us that push to keep playing until the end. That was the most important thing. It was one of the best games for all the supporters, for myself and for Jürgen. To have played for him was a pleasure and I'll never forget it. He is special, like a Messi or a Salah, and there have not been many others like him. In 100 years, people will still be speaking about the Jürgen Klopp era at Liverpool. He leaves behind a massive legacy, not just at Anfield, but in football generally. Everyone will miss him."

DEJAN LOVREN

colour filled the stands, yellow and black in one corner, red and white everywhere else, while noise levels barely dipped below ear-piercing.

It really was a spectacle to savour and the fact it was 'only' the Europa League on a Thursday night didn't matter. This was a game of great importance. Having been eliminated from the FA Cup in a fourth-round replay at West Ham, it was Liverpool's last chance at silverware that season and, with it, their most likely passage back to the Champions League, given they were also nine points adrift of the top four in the Premier League. For Dortmund, it was the only European trophy they had yet to win.

In his pre-match press conference, opposition coach Thomas Tuchel had vowed that his team would attack and they certainly did, leaving Klopp to watch helplessly from the sidelines as the visitors raced into a shock 2-0 lead within the opening nine minutes.

With away goals counting double, Liverpool now needed to score three. Not since the 2005 Champions League Final had a Liverpool team faced such a daunting task. Dortmund, yet to be beaten in 2016, were in total control and seemingly sailing towards a place in the last four.

During the half-time break, Klopp knew he had to lift the sagging spirits of his players. He pointed to the club's legendary Champions League Final comeback in Istanbul as a prime example that nothing was impossible and urged them to create a moment they could tell their grandchildren about in years to come.

Three minutes into the second half, Origi scored, only for the renewed sense of hope to be quickly deflated when Dortmund netted a third goal. Liverpool were

back to the position where they'd started the half and, with time ticking, faced the almightiest of uphill struggles, the likes of which had never been accomplished at Anfield before.

For many, it was now a case of damage limitation, but when Philippe Coutinho pulled a goal back in the 66th minute, belief was restored. With the crowd roused and Liverpool attacking the Kop, Klopp urged his team to keep pushing forward. It paid off when Mamadou Sakho headed home to make it 3-3 with 12 minutes remaining. The stands shook and the volume was cranked up another notch, but as time drifted towards 90 minutes, Dortmund were still heading through on away goals.

As the fourth official's board lit up to show that four minutes of injury time were to be played, the action became even more frantic and the atmosphere more frenzied. From a free-kick just inside their opponents' half, Daniel Sturridge and James Milner combined down the right, with the latter delivering a pinpoint cross deep towards the far post. Dejan Lovren rose highest to plant a header into the roof of the net. Cue bedlam.

Anfield exploded. Lovren slid on his knees in celebration and Klopp went ballistic. "Liverpool have come back from the dead," roared the television commentator, and it was the manager who had breathed this new life into them, a never-say-die spirit that would become the hallmark of his time at the club.

Ahead of schedule, Klopp had succeeded in giving the new generation of supporters their own moment of history to cherish. There would be plenty more to come but the first will always remain special.

Above left:
Dejan Lovren slides away in celebration after his last-gasp header secures a dramatic victory.

Above right:
Jürgen can't contain his delight and reacts with a trademark fist pump.

SWISS SETBACK

Liverpool v Sevilla | Europa League Final, 18 May 2016

If reaching the League Cup Final at Wembley was seen as the first major step forward in Liverpool's revival under Jürgen Klopp, repeating that run in the Europa League was an even more impressive feat.

While domestic fortunes are still regarded as the 'bread and butter' at Anfield, it's success in Europe that stirs the emotions of Liverpool's fanbase more than anything else. The progress made by Klopp's team in the knockout rounds of the Europa League had lit a fuse. To be back in a European final so soon into the new manager's reign was an unexpected but much welcomed bonus.

All roads now led to the St Jakob Park Arena in Basel for a final showdown with Sevilla.

"Europe is big," said Klopp, "and a lot of teams want to go to finals. It's not too easy. Now we are there. It's a great opportunity."

Below: The red flags and scarves were out in force ahead of the 2016 Europa League Final.

As is the tradition, Liverpool supporters made the trek in massive numbers, despite the stadium being nowhere near big enough to accommodate everyone. They draped their well-worn flags and banners from every vantage point they could find to make it feel like home from home for the manager and his players.

It was all set up for a fitting finale to Klopp's first season at the club. Given the run they had enjoyed in the competition, no-one could deny that Liverpool deserved to be here, but this would be a much sterner test than the one faced against Villarreal in the semi-final. Sevilla had been the dominant force in this competition for years, winning it a record number of times, and they were aiming for a third successive triumph.

Liverpool started well enough and looked on course for victory after Daniel Sturridge's sublime finish ten minutes before half-time broke the deadlock. What followed was a second-half capitulation that was difficult to explain. Sevilla drew level within a minute of the restart, then added a further two goals to shatter the silver-lined finish Klopp had hoped for. "It was obvious their first goal was a big influence on our game. We lost faith in our style of play, and I am responsible for this performance," was his honest post-match assessment.

The pain of defeat cut deep, but back at the team hotel later that night, the manager insisted beers were drunk and songs were sung. Klopp was beaten but refused to be broken, and he made sure his players felt the same.

The Europa League Final had ultimately proved a step too far, one game too many in what had been a long but pivotal season. The new era would have to wait for its first trophy, but Jürgen Klopp remained defiant: "I promise everybody we will use it and come back stronger. I am sure we will be in another final, and next time we know we have to do better."

Above left:
Emre Can attempts to thwart a dangerous Sevilla attack.

Above right:
Despite a spectacular first-half strike, Daniel Sturridge is a forlorn figure at the final whistle.

Next page:
Down but not out: Jürgen applauds the fans and promises Liverpool will be back.

"We were all really down after this game,
and I remember being back at the hotel when
I got a call to say we needed to be downstairs.
No-one was in the mood but when we got there
Jürgen was on the dancefloor urging everyone
to get up and join him. We were all looking
at each other, thinking, 'What is he doing?' but
everyone was soon up on the stage dancing.
It ended up being one of the best parties I've
ever been to. That summed up Jürgen for me.
You sensed straight away with him that he
was a guy you could trust. The way he spoke,
the way he managed a dressing room, even
the way he shook your hand. It was just
different. Everyone was immediately on board
with him, and it came as no surprise to see
what he went on to achieve."

KOLO TOURE

FROM DOUBTERS TO BELIEVERS

2016–18

STARTING GUN

Arsenal v Liverpool | Premier League, 14 August 2016

Club-record signing Sadio Mané on his Liverpool debut, getting a piggy-back off manager Jürgen Klopp after scoring at the Emirates on the opening day of the 2016/17 season: as goal celebrations go, it has to be among the most bizarre.

It came in a game that typified the unpredictable, roller-coaster nature of the early days of Klopp's Liverpool team. Despite reaching two cup finals the previous season, they had failed to mount a challenge for Champions League qualification and eventually finished 8th, 11 points behind runners-up Arsenal.

In the 63rd minute, Mané cut in from the right and beat two defenders before unleashing an unstoppable shot into the far top corner. It was an early Goal of the

Season contender. More importantly, it gave Liverpool a seemingly unassailable 4-1 lead.

With Ragnar Klavan and Gini Wijnaldum also making their debuts, Liverpool had conceded first, when Theo Walcott netted for the hosts moments after missing a first-half penalty. On the stroke of half-time, Philippe Coutinho levelled with a stunning free-kick, before three goals delivered in 14 minutes during the second half – from Adam Lallana, Coutinho again then Mané – looked to have put the game to bed.

That's certainly what Klopp thought as amid the mayhem of the fourth goal he invited the celebrating Senegal striker to jump on his back in triumph. Little did he know that this game was not yet over. Despite the summer signings of Klavan and Joel Matip, the fragility of Liverpool's back line, which had been exposed on several occasions during Klopp's first season, had still not been fully rectified and poor defending allowed Arsenal to pull two back, leaving the visitors to nervously hold on for a thrilling 4-3 win.

Reflecting on the moment for which the game is best remembered, Klopp acknowledged he was at fault for celebrating like he did, explaining: "I made a mistake and played a big part in the excitement of the last half-hour, because it's not allowed to celebrate the fourth goal like this with 35 minutes to go. At this moment, we switched off the machines. The game was not over. Arsenal lost, but we gave them a path back into the game. Nothing is sure until the final whistle."

Opposite:
New signing Sadio Mané celebrates scoring on his debut by jumping on Jürgen's back.

Above left:
Roberto Firmino and Arsenal's Rob Holding in aerial combat at the Emirates Stadium.

Above right:
Sadio Mané's impact at Liverpool was instant and the Gunners' defence struggled to contain him.

"He arrived with a good reputation and justified it. The first impression I had of him was a guy who is a strong character, who knows what he wants, who can dictate his ideas and convince people of what he thinks his right. He regenerated Liverpool, aligning the culture of his team with the culture of the city. You could see early on, his impact on the team, in the fighting spirit, in the desire not to lose and the refusal to lie down when it didn't go well. You could see already that Liverpool could be a threat. A team is always a reflection of the manager's personality and the behaviour of never giving up is certainly a trait of Jürgen's. His career has been based on the important qualities of integrity, commitment, loyalty and respect. He remained true to these and dedicated his life to the job."

ARSENE WENGER

From threatening to run out emphatic winners, to recklessly almost throwing away the points, it had been another 90 minutes of fluctuating emotions. No wonder Liverpool were a prime 'pick' for the television broadcasters. To the watching neutrals, it made for compelling viewing, but the manager was well aware of the need to rectify the issues that were continuing to plague his team. "Scoring four is wonderful, conceding three is the opposite," he said. "It gives us the confidence and knowledge that we can score goals, but we have to defend better together."

Nevertheless, to get his first full season off to a flying start with an away win over Arsene Wenger's Arsenal, no matter how it was achieved, was no mean feat. "It was hard work, but a brilliant win. A deserved win," concluded the boss.

As for Klopp's now famous piggy-back celebration, it was later voted fourth in the top ten Liverpool goal celebrations of 2016/17, but never repeated.

Above:
Despite a late rally by the hosts, Liverpool hung on to claim an impressive opening day win.

THE SCOUSER IN OUR TEAM

Liverpool v Tottenham Hotspur | League Cup 4th round, 25 October 2016

Trent Alexander-Arnold was a tall and gangly kid, just 17 years of age when Jürgen Klopp first set eyes on him. It was during a Liverpool under-18s game at the club's Academy in Kirkby. "I like what I see in this player," said the manager, who immediately earmarked him as one for the future. Within a year Alexander-Arnold was a first-team player.

Raised in the Clubmoor area of the city, Alexander-Arnold had first come to the attention of Liverpool scouts after being selected by his school to attend a summer training camp arranged by the club.

He was a boyhood Red who grew up wanting to be the next Steven Gerrard and played like him too. Scouts from Everton and Manchester United were also circling but there was only ever one club Alexander-Arnold wanted to be at.

Below: A young Trent Alexander-Arnold in action for Liverpool under-18s at the club's Academy.

Liverpool carefully monitored his progress as a player with local junior team Country Park and signed him up to start training under their watchful eye at the Academy when he was just six years of age. The young Alexander-Arnold rose steadily through the ranks and was highly rated by his coaches at Kirkby.

An England youth international, he captained the club's under-16 and under-18 sides.

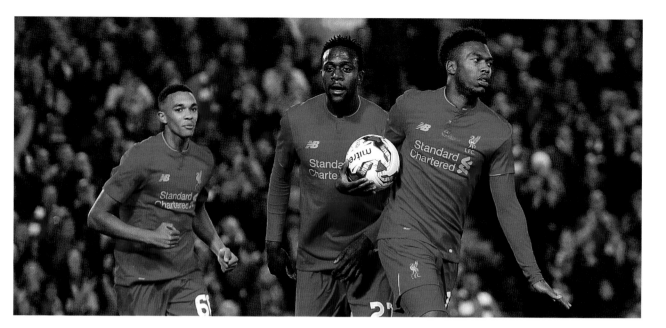

Klopp recognised his potential straight away, inviting him to train with the first team, taking him on the 2016 summer tour and naming him as an unused substitute in Liverpool's opening Premier League game of the season away to Arsenal.

"He was a big talent," remembered the boss. "When you saw him, wow, football-wise no doubts but we were not sure he could do it physically. He was a kid and not fit enough. So, we had to work on that, but then he made steps by himself that were unbelievable."

Klopp has never been afraid to give youth a chance, especially in the earlier rounds of cup competitions. Two weeks after turning 18, Alexander-Arnold got his opportunity in the League Cup fourth round tie at home to Tottenham.

Wearing the number 66 shirt for the first time and lining up at right-back, he was then the youngest player to be handed a debut by Klopp. Despite being booked for an early foul, he repaid the manager's faith in him with an impressive performance in Liverpool's 2-1 win.

"You need to come back in the game when you have difficult moments, like the yellow card," Klopp said. "He had to stay in the game with a lot of challenges on the wing and do it smart. That's a really good sign."

With the manager's help, a big future beckoned for Anfield's latest rising teenage star. His first-team breakthrough was rewarded with a new contract and a Premier League debut soon followed. He later became the first Scouser since Gerrard to fully establish himself in the team and evolved into one of the world's finest right-backs.

Not bad for a normal lad from Liverpool. Under Jürgen Klopp, Alexander-Arnold would live the dream.

Above:
A teenage Trent Alexander-Arnold slotted in seamlessly on his first-team debut.

Next page:
A graduate of the club's Academy, Trent Alexander-Arnold is an inspiration for all young players.

"Within his first few weeks, Jürgen was down at the Academy watching the young lads and this gave us all a massive boost. It was a statement to the club that he was willing to give youth a chance, one I benefited from so much. The day before the Tottenham game he told me to make sure my family was there because I was going to start. He said it was going to be a proud moment but not to overthink things, to relax, stay calm and get as much sleep as possible. He also explained that I should just play as I'd been training, that I had earned the opportunity and that I was ready. As a young player, it's the best thing you can be told and everything he said I took into the game with me. Without Jürgen, who knows how my career would have panned out?"

TRENT ALEXANDER-ARNOLD

MANÉ SCORING

Everton v Liverpool | Premier League, 19 December 2016

The Christmas festivities started early for one half of Merseyside in 2016 and the red plumes of smoke that billowed out from a small corner of Goodison Park were a clue to which side was celebrating.

Just 0.8 miles separate the home grounds of Liverpool and Everton, and the red mist could still be seen wafting over Stanley Park in the direction of Anfield as supporters headed back to toast their team's reaffirmed status as the undisputed pride of their city.

This was Jürgen Klopp's first experience of that short trip 'across the park' and it was one that won't be forgotten. The previous season he celebrated his derby debut by overseeing an emphatic 4-0 annihilation of the Blues, but that was at Anfield.

Going into this 227th episode of a local spat that had been playing out since 1893, the Reds were third in the table, 11 points ahead of Everton in 9th, but as the old saying goes, form counts for nothing in these games.

Below: Jürgen leads his team at Goodison Park for the first time alongside opposite number Ronald Koeman.

It had also been five years since Liverpool supporters had been able to celebrate a victory in front of the Gwladys Street. Brendan Rodgers had failed on each of his four attempts, and it was in the aftermath of the corresponding fixture a season before that the decision was made to dispense with his services.

That was a game Klopp had watched on television, just days before receiving the call that would change his life. As a self-confessed fan of the Rocky movie franchise, he admitted to preparing for this match by watching *Creed*, the latest spin-off in the series and one that, to his surprise, culminated with a fight scene at Goodison.

It all added to the unique build-up, which, given the close proximity of the two clubs, was unlike anything he had encountered in Germany. "I'm [now] part of Liverpool so it is really easy for me to accept the importance of the game. I like how Liverpool the city lives with these two big clubs and it will be very special to be at Goodison for the first time," he said.

There proved to be little to separate the sides. The game was deadlocked at 0-0 deep into stoppage time when substitute Daniel Sturridge tried his luck with a low shot from just outside the box. It wasn't a particularly powerful strike, but it beat the keeper and bounced back off the post. Sadio Mané reacted quickest to knock the ball over the line from close range and snatch an incredible last-gasp win.

"Great, intense, how a derby should be," was Klopp's immediate post-match reaction. "Not the best football in the world, of course, but you can't ignore the intensity and importance of a game like this. You have to take it like it is. Second half, we took it like it should be."

Jürgen Klopp had passed another important test in his role as Liverpool manager and given supporters the Christmas present they craved most. If he wasn't already an adopted Scouser, he was well on his way to becoming one.

Above: With virtually the last kick of the game Sadio Mané pounces to clinch the points.

Next page: The matchwinner runs off to receive the acclaim of the jubilant Liverpool supporters.

"Since day one when I first spoke to him about joining Liverpool, we had a really good relationship, and he very much helped me become the player I did. We enjoyed so many great times together and would become the best in the world but games like when I scored the late winner at Everton were also special and an important part of that journey. We didn't play well in the first half that night and he told us at half-time to keep things simple and be patient. It gave us confidence that a goal would come, and he was right. That goal meant a lot to the fans and I'm thankful to Jürgen for enabling me to enjoy this moment, plus so many more. He is a great manager, with a big heart, and was totally dedicated to making the team successful. It's what made him so special."

SADIO MANÉ

"He's the coach who brought me here and gave me the opportunity to play for this wonderful club so, of course, he's had a great impact on my career. Coming to a new country is not easy but I learnt a lot from his general outlook on life and the way he sees football. Getting into the Champions League was important for our development and securing qualification was a great way to end my first season at Liverpool. He was determined to get the club back playing at the highest level and it showed the direction we were heading. We went on to spend many more years together. He made me a better player and it's hard to imagine playing for another manager at Liverpool. Wearing the red shirt always gave me a sense of pride and Jürgen Klopp had a lot to do with that."

JOEL MATIP

BACK IN THE BIG TIME

Liverpool v Middlesbrough | Premier League, 21 May 2017

The days of 'first is first, second is nothing' had long gone. Entering the final weekend of the 2016/17 Premier League season, the prize Liverpool had their eye on was a third- or fourth-place finish that would take them back to the promised land of Europe's elite competition.

It had been the number one priority for Jürgen Klopp since he'd taken charge at the club and was imperative for his future plans. Three years had elapsed since Anfield last hosted Champions League football and the next phase of his rebuilding project hinged on it.

"Liverpool need to be there consistently," said the manager. "We should do everything to change this. It is the best tournament in Europe. There is nothing better, maybe, in the world. You want to be there. We will be really strong and fight for it."

Klopp's first full season therefore had all been about the league. A title challenge may have been expecting too much, but his team did top the table for a spell in November and were consistently close to the top four.

Above: Jürgen in front of the Main Stand at Anfield on a day when victory was essential.

Come the final game, Chelsea had long since wrapped up the title, but fourth-placed Liverpool still had plenty to play for, with the battle for the remaining two Champions League places going down to the wire. Manchester City, in third, were still within reach, but it was Arsenal, a point behind in fifth, who posed the threat. Liverpool could settle for nothing less than a win.

Standing in their way was an already relegated Middlesbrough, yet the stakes couldn't have been higher. For much of the first half, nerves seemed to have got the better of the Reds and, as half-time approached, they were struggling to make a breakthrough. In North London, Arsenal were winning.

"Champions League? You're having a laugh," sang the visiting fans at Anfield but those taunts were suddenly silenced when, in first-half stoppage time, Gini Wijnaldum scored. Within six minutes of the restart Philippe Coutinho had doubled the advantage, then Adam Lallana netted another. On the touchline, Klopp was

celebrating by wildly grinding his teeth and beating his chest. "I'm really happy about this," he said afterwards. "What a wonderful day."

Above:
The players celebrate Adam Lallana's goal as a top-four finish is secured.

The fact that Manchester City also won meant Liverpool finished fourth and would have to face a two-legged qualifier before their Champions League return was fully assured, but the manager wasn't too stressed about that.

This is what he had set out to achieve at the start of the season and his project remained on track. Summer signings Wijnaldum, Sadio Mané and Joel Matip had all played their part and the ranks could now be bolstered again in readiness for the new challenges ahead. "I'm really looking forward to next season," Klopp added. "I think we have created a wonderful base."

As a previous Anfield manager once said, European football without Liverpool is like a banquet without wine. For Jürgen Klopp's Liverpool, a veritable feast lay in store.

EGYPTIAN KING

The signing of Mohamed Salah, 22 June 2017

At first glance Mo Salah appeared to be an unlikely transfer target for Liverpool in the summer of 2017. When news of their interest in him first surfaced, more than a few eyebrows were raised.

Jürgen Klopp, however, had been a long-timer admirer of Salah. He once tried to sign him for Borussia Dortmund and the Egyptian forward had remained on his radar ever since. "He was at Basel when we played them, and we didn't know him. It was like 'what the f**k'. It was unbelievable," recalled Klopp. "Then the moment I said, 'let's go for him', he'd already gone to Chelsea."

That was in 2014. Ironically, Liverpool were also interested in signing Salah back then, but his brief spell at Stamford Bridge had the critics doubting the wisdom of their move for him now. Not that Klopp allowed this to cloud his judgement. "He struggled at Chelsea because it was too early. He was a kid. We all need confidence. We all need help from outside, especially as a young player in a foreign, very strong, very demanding league."

Brought to England by Jose Mourinho, Salah's impact was admittedly minimal, scoring just twice in 19 appearances at Chelsea. One of those games was at Anfield – in the infamous game that ultimately robbed Liverpool of the 2013/14 Premier League title. Frustrated that he was unable to get the best out of him, Mourinho then sent Salah out on loan to Italy. First to Fiorentina then to Roma, with a permanent switch to the latter eventually completed in 2016.

With the Giallorossi, Salah's reputation soared, capturing the attention of the Liverpool scouts. What attracted them was Salah's versatility as an offensive player, whether that was operating in midfield, on the wing or up front. He had pace to burn and skills to match, a creator of goals and a taker of goals. These attributes would suit Klopp's quick counter-pressing style. The scouting reports on him after his performance for Roma in 2016/17 were filed away under the category 'complete package'.

Klopp wasn't originally 100 per cent sure of whether Salah was still the right player for Liverpool at this exact time, though. He credits the club's scouting department with having to convince him: "They did a fantastic job around Mo. They just didn't get out of our ears about him. It was '100 percent he is ready, he is ready'."

Klopp's concern focused on whether Salah possessed the physical and mental strength to handle life in the Premier League. "His speed, that is clear but of course we had to look at a lot of his games to see about other parts. Physicality, being strong enough for challenges. If you watch him only on television, he looks quite skinny." After meeting him in person for the first time though, the manager's mind was made up and he understood what his scouts had been telling him. Klopp now agreed. "He looked ready."

The size of the fee was a big talking point, but once negotiations were concluded and Salah had put pen to paper on his record-breaking deal to become the club's first major close-season signing, the boss was delighted. "We know what we are getting. His record in Italy was outstanding and he possesses qualities that will enhance our team and squad. He is a really exciting signing for us. And we are really happy we could convince him to come here.

"Mohamed has the perfect mix of experience and potential. He knows the Premier League; he has pedigree in the Champions League, and he is one of the most important players for his country. I have followed him since he emerged at Basel, and he has matured into a really good player. His pace is incredible, he gives us more attacking threat and we are already strong in this area. I like that we will make it even more competitive.

"Most important though, for us, is that he is hungry, willing and eager to be even better and improve further. He believes in what we are trying to do here at

Below:
Mo Salah puts pen to paper on the deal that makes him a Liverpool player.

Above:
Mo Salah nets
on his Premier
League debut
for the Reds at
Vicarage Road.

Liverpool and is extremely keen to be part of it. He is an ambitious player who wants to win and win at the highest level; he knows he can fulfil those ambitions with Liverpool."

The feeling was mutual and Salah himself told the club's official website: "I'm very excited to be here. I'm very happy. I will give 100 per cent and give everything for the club. I really want to win something for this club. We have a great team and very good players. Everyone can see the coach gives everything. I hope to see that together we can give everything to win something for the club, for the supporters and for us."

Klopp set his new signing no targets in terms of how many goals he expected from him, but no-one could have predicted just how many Salah would net over the course of the next seven years.

A couple of weeks after officially becoming a Liverpool player, he got off the mark in a friendly away to Wigan Athletic and went on to register another three during pre-season. On the opening day of the 2017/18 Premier League campaign, Salah then celebrated his official debut by scoring the third in a 3-3 draw against Watford at Vicarage Road. From that moment on, he didn't look back. No goalscoring record was safe.

"Jürgen and I shared the same goal, which was winning trophies for this club, and, of course, that had an influence on my decision to come here. We had a good conversation, he told me about his plans for the team and convinced me that Liverpool was the team for me. Ever since I joined we have always had a good relationship. We got to know each other very well, appreciate each other and respect each other. We also did everything we could to help each other win things, which has been the most important thing. We didn't have success straight away but I'm so proud that, together, we went on to achieve all that we did. The boss improved everything during his time here, everybody loved him and he's been a great manager, that's plain to see. It's been incredible to play for him."

MO SALAH

CALM AS YOU LIKE

The signing of Virgil van Dijk, 1 January 2018

The best things come to those who wait, but Jürgen Klopp had to have the patience of a saint to complete what would be one of his and the club's most important ever signings.

Having reinforced his attacking options with the club-record capture of Mo Salah, Klopp knew it was equally important to now bolster the defence. Dejan Lovren and Joel Matip had shown promise as a centre-back pairing and been on the losing side in just one of the 18 games they started together the previous season. But Liverpool still conceded more goals than the three sides that finished above them in the table. He'd brought in full-back Andy Robertson from Hull City, but knew that a new centre-half with real leadership qualities was crucial to his future plans. Southampton captain Virgil van Dijk would be his number one target.

"In that moment he was the most wanted centre-half in England," remembers Klopp. "In the two years he played at Southampton before he got injured, that was really incredible. I saw something of him at Celtic, but I didn't see this world-class player, already. I saw a very-good centre-half, but I didn't need one at that time. And then when we needed him in the moment, it was clear, he can make the next step with us."

With Manchester City and Chelsea also interested and the Saints reluctant to sell, the deal was never going to be easy, but it proved to be one of the most protracted transfer sagas in history.

There was a significant vulnerability about Liverpool's defense; Jürgen Klopp believed that Van Dijk could be the talisman for a glorious new era at Anfield and wanted to sign him during the summer transfer window. Southampton, though, were adamant that Van Dijk was not for sale and the transfer window ended without a deal. A long list of alternative options were discussed, but Klopp was adamant that the big Dutchman was the only player he wanted. "There was no-one really who was better," remained the manager's stance.

He decided to wait, but it was still a huge gamble by the boss, one that drew some understandable concern among the fanbase. Some believed he was right to bide his time, others feared his decision could have an adverse effect on the team's chances of success that season.

During the first half of 2017/18, it was the latter who had more reason to feel

"When joining a club, the most important thing you look at is the manager – and Jürgen Klopp was one of the main reasons I chose Liverpool. From the first moment we spoke, he sold the club to me. I sat, listened and thought, 'This just sounds like the perfect fit for me'. The boss has something special about him, that's for sure, but what I think he possesses more than others is his man-management. These days that is so important in football. He fills the team with confidence and pushes them forward, while individually, he just gives you this great feeling that really inspires you as a player. I sensed it straight away in my first game. I wasn't due to play originally but he changed his mind and I'm so glad he did because it was an unforgettable night for me. The start of something special."

VIRGIL VAN DIJK

vindicated. Three or more goals were conceded in a game on five occasions.

For a team again sitting on the periphery of the title race and making hard work of qualifying from the group phase of the Champions League, it was a worry that only served to strengthen Klopp's resolve to secure Van Dijk. He firmly believed that, with him in the side, Liverpool would be capable of taking that all-important next step.

Klopp never gave up and eventually, between Christmas and New Year, a deal was finally struck. It required yet another club record fee, but a delighted Klopp had got his man at last.

"We wanted Virg in the summer but couldn't do the transfer, then in the winter we tried again and got it through. It was very important and changed a lot for us. When Virgil made his decision, it was a fantastic day. A big day in our history and a massive statement."

Van Dijk was a modern-day colossus and a throwback to former Liverpool skipper Ron Yeats, upon whom the success of Bill Shankly's first great team had been built. Klopp stopped short of inviting journalists to 'walk around him', as Shankly had done with Yeats back in 1962, but the impact of his signing would have similar connotations.

Handed the number four shirt, Van Dijk couldn't wait to walk in such legendary footsteps and pull on the famous red shirt. "With the history at the club, the manager, supporters and everything around it, it is just a perfect, perfect match for me, and the right time for me to be here," he explained.

Just four days later, the club's new centre-half was pitched straight into the frenzied atmosphere of a Merseyside derby at Anfield. It was an FA Cup third-round tie on a freezing Friday night and Klopp admitted he deliberated over whether to play him.

"It was a spontaneous decision. In the morning, I actually thought he will not play. It's not that I didn't want him to play, but it was the first game, against Everton. If something goes in the wrong direction it's not a cool start and we want a good start for him. But then I thought he's ready for it, so we did it and it was a genius decision."

In a fiercely contested battle, Van Dijk duly delivered. The debutant oozed class and composure from the first minute, comfortably winning his aerial duels and using the ball intelligently. James Milner opened the scoring with a first-half penalty before Everton drew level after the break. Then, six minutes from time, with a replay increasingly likely, from a corner on the left the towering centre-back rose majestically above the blue shirts and powered a header into the Kop net.

It couldn't have been scripted any better. Anfield erupted and the supporters

instantly had themselves a new hero. "Expectation can lead to pressure. He obviously could stand the pressure. It's a fairy tale and there are not a lot of fairy tales in the world any more," hailed Klopp afterwards.

After just one game, both the long wait to sign Van Dijk and the record outlay it required were looking well worth it. He was the new defensive rock of Jürgen Klopp's Liverpool, and much more. Before too long, everyone would be singing about him.

Above:
Virgil van Dijk's Liverpool career got off to a perfect start with victory over Everton at Anfield.

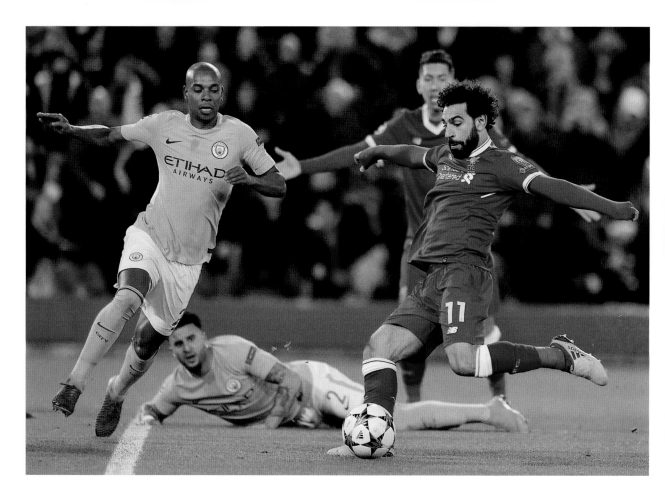

A TALE OF TWO CITY'S

Liverpool v Manchester City | Champions League quarter-final 1st leg, 4 April 2018

The roots of a rivalry that is now considered one of the biggest in English football can be traced back to an unforgettable European night at Anfield in April 2018.

Until this point, despite their close geographical proximity, Liverpool and Manchester City had co-existed fairly peacefully. Any enmity directed down the M62 was traditionally aimed at those of a United persuasion, and vice-versa. Understandable given their status as the country's two most successful clubs.

City, however, were now on the rise. Since they pipped Liverpool to the League Cup on penalties two seasons before, Pep Guardiola had taken over at the Etihad and would lead them to the Premier League title in the 2018/2019 season.

Klopp and Guardiola were no strangers. They had been rivals in Germany at their respective former clubs in Dortmund and Munich. Both were considered among the brightest managerial talents in the game, and Klopp had nothing but

praise for his opposite number. "I really respect him a lot. I really think he is the best manager in the world."

Table-topping City harboured serious hopes of going all the way in the competition for the first time and were favourites to progress. It was exactly the type of challenge Klopp thrived on. "What they do, they do at the highest level, but we know there's a chance. And that's the only thing I need."

City were in for a rude awakening. An ear-splitting crescendo and rampant red tide engulfed the shell-shocked visitors from the first minute.

Liverpool burst out of the starting blocks and punished their opponents for forcing them to attack the Kop in the first half. Klopp's high-press tactics ensured City had no time to settle and before they knew it their Champions League aspirations had all but evaporated into the Mersey. "You have no alternative if you want to beat City," explained Klopp. "You could sit deep in your box and hope nothing happens, but we are Liverpool, and we should try to win this way."

Mo Salah, with his 38th strike of what was turning into a highly prolific first season at the club, inflicted the first blow. Fellow summer recruit Alex

Opposite: Mo Salah opens the scoring against Manchester City on a memorable European night at Anfield.

Above: Alex Oxlade-Chamberlain doubles Liverpool's advantage on their way to a famous 3-0 win.

"A very special personality with such charisma, such an energy and the capacity to inspire a club. He completely transformed it in a way that united the whole club. You could sense it on day one. How confident he looked, the words he used, the way he was connecting with people straight away, the relationship with the fans and players. He was made for that journey. From a tactical aspect a lot of our headaches were related to how you are going to break the press. They were a really intense, really effective side at winning the ball high up the pitch and when they did that you knew what was going to happen. You're going to be on the back foot in open spaces against three very fast players that are going to cause you problems. He brought something very different to the Premier League. A monumental influence on English football."

MIKEL ARTETA

Oxlade-Chamberlain quickly added a second before Sadio Mané chipped in to make it 3-0 just after the half-hour mark.

There was no further scoring, but the damage had been done. Scarves twirled in celebration as Liverpool supporters revelled in a victory that they could never have imagined would be so emphatic. "We beat the best team in the world," claimed Klopp afterwards.

The formalities of the tie were completed in Manchester the following week. The champions-elect had been put firmly in their place and an ominous warning had been issued that something serious was brewing at Anfield with Klopp at the helm.

A red force had been reawakened, but Guardiola and City, still smarting from this defeat, would loom large in Liverpool's quest for success over the next few seasons. A new rivalry had been ignited.

Above:
The manager and his captain applaud the fans at the end of the quarter-final 1st leg.

ARRIVEDERCI ROMA

Liverpool v AS Roma | Champions League semi-final 2nd leg, 2 May 2018

Being the location of European Cup wins in 1977 and 1984, for Liverpudlians, there is no place like Rome. The capital of Italy will always command a special place in their hearts. A succession of legendary Liverpool managers had triumphed here: Bob Paisley, Joe Fagan and Gerard Houllier. Hence why, just as the Romans do, Scousers really believe it is the Eternal City. In the spring of 2018, Jürgen Klopp's name was about to join this illustrious list.

With a defender called Virgil among his ranks, perhaps it was fated, for it was a poet by the same name who originally described Rome as 'an empire without end'. Locals believed that even if the empire fell, the city would last forever. Liverpool supporters believed similarly about their club, and Klopp was their new emperor.

Just as they had done many times before, Liverpool were once again the country's standard bearers in Europe. On what was their first appearance back in the Champions League since 2014, their run to the last four had been as unexpected as it had been exhilarating.

Boosted by the defensive stability that new signing Virgil van Dijk brought to the team, their form had improved immeasurably during the second half of the campaign. Domestically, it still wasn't sufficient to challenge runaway Premier League leaders Manchester City, but it saw them power through the first two knockout rounds of the continent's most coveted competition.

The transformation under Klopp had been a remarkable one. In just over two years he had taken a team seemingly anchored in mediocrity to the brink of a final that Liverpool had not graced for 11 years, and the red flag was flying high once again.

Not only that, he had changed people's view of Liverpool. Going into this semi-final, their right to be rubbing shoulders with the cream of the continent was no longer being doubted. The mighty Reds of Europe, as the song goes, were back where they belonged.

There were two incredibly intriguing subplots in the build-up to this massive tie. Firstly, followers of semi-final opponents AS Roma had never forgotten the pain of losing on home soil to Liverpool in 1984 and being denied a first-ever European title. Alan Kennedy's winning penalty in the shoot-out that night left an indelible stain on their history. Over three decades had passed but they still talked about one day avenging that defeat.

"Getting Liverpool back into the Champions League was a big achievement but Jürgen was never content to just be part of the competition. If his team were in it, they were in it to win it and we enjoyed a great run to the final at our first attempt here. He was gradually turning the club around and we were pretty confident going to Rome. Of course, no game there is ever going to be easy and Jürgen was quick to remind everyone that they had to approach the second leg as if the tie was still goalless. He didn't like the fact that we eventually lost the game but knowing we were through to another final was a great moment and a further sign of the progress being made. Jürgen is a natural leader who didn't rest for one second in his quest to bring success back to Anfield."

PETER KRAWIETZ

Another was Mo Salah's reunion with his former club, just under a year after he'd last worn a Roma shirt.

In the first leg at Anfield, Salah was on fire, scoring twice and providing two assists as a rampant Liverpool swept the Romans away. At 5-0 with 68 minutes played, a record score at this stage of the competition very much appeared a possibility. With the action still unfolding in front of them, supporters could have been forgiven for scanning the internet in search of cheap flights to Kyiv for the final.

When Roma managed to hit back with two late goals in the last nine minutes, though, and almost got a third, it may not have seemed such a good idea. Adding to the air of caution was the fact that the Italians had fought back from a similar deficit in the quarter-final against Barcelona.

Ahead of the second leg in Rome a week later, Klopp remained quietly confident. "We were very positive at Anfield and then after the game a few people had the feeling that we lost, but we didn't. We are in a much better situation than I could have imagined. Much better."

Asked how his team would be set up to approach the game, he added: "There is no perfect plan for it. If you really want to win, you have to accept first that you could lose. We need to be brave and use their situation more than they use their

Below:
AS Roma goalkeeper Alisson Becker shields the ball from his future team-mate Mo Salah.

situation because they have to win against us, and they have to take risks. We have to use that."

The Stadio Olimpico in Rome can be an intimidating arena, but when Sadio Mané fired Liverpool ahead after just nine minutes of the return, any pre-match doubts seemed to have been eased. James Milner scored for Roma shortly after, but it wasn't long before Georginio Wijnaldum restored the advantage.

However, the night was still young. Roma reduced the aggregate deficit early in the second half then, four minutes from time, edged in front. Requiring two more to draw level, time was against Roma, but when they scored from a penalty in the final minute, the nerves of the away fans began to jangle.

From what had been a position of relative comfort, a tiring Liverpool were now suddenly hanging on, desperate to avoid an added half hour. "It was a little bit exciting, more exciting than I actually wanted," admitted Klopp. "It was the first time we were not really as good as we can be, and I don't know how we would have coped with extra time."

Thankfully, Liverpool weathered the storm, so he didn't have to find out. The final whistle sparked joyous scenes among the players on the pitch and the 5,000 vociferous travelling supporters in the stands.

The manager later conceded that good fortune had favoured his team at times but was relieved and thrilled to have taken them through to the final. "We had a bit of luck and we needed it but over the whole campaign it's deserved. We came into the competition as a qualifier and now we are in the final, so I'm delighted."

Determined to savour this special moment, Klopp re-emerged from the dressing room 30 minutes later to celebrate in front of the fans once more. "These people followed us all over Europe. Seeing their happy faces is the best thing football can do."

Liverpool had lost the battle but won the war. Rome had been conquered yet again and Jürgen Klopp's Red army was marching on towards its next crusade.

Above left:
Sadio Mané celebrates with the travelling Liverpudlians as a place in the final is secured.

Above right:
Jürgen's joy is clear to see as the final whistle blows in Rome's Stadio Olimpico.

ONE KISS

Liverpool v Real Madrid | Champions League Final, 26 May 2018

To truly appreciate the good times, you must first endure the bad. But, on what should have been a glorious night in Ukraine, that would have been of little consolation to Jürgen Klopp after experiencing his lowest point yet as Liverpool manager.

It was the grand climax to a season in which Klopp had succeeded in fully turning supporters from doubters to believers. The team's run to a first Champions League Final in over a decade had convinced everybody that this team was heading in the right direction and that they had the potential to emulate some of the great Liverpool sides of the past.

In Mo Salah, the Reds could boast one of the most feared finishers on the continent. From a personal perspective, his debut season at the club couldn't have gone any better. After scoring on his first appearance, he continued to hit the back of the net at an impressive rate, notching a record 32 goals in the Premier League to claim the Golden Boot, the first Liverpool player to do so since Luis Suarez in 2014.

In Europe, his 11 goals had been instrumental in firing Liverpool towards the final and the attacking triumvirate he spearheaded alongside Roberto Firmino and Sadio Mané was fast developing into one of the most exciting ever seen at Anfield.

Below:
Liverpool supporters in Kyiv for the 2018 Champions League Final against Real Madrid.

Of Klopp's other recent recruits, Virgil van Dijk had slotted in seamlessly at the back, bringing with him a calmness that had been missing, Andy Robertson had made the left-back position his own, while Alex Oxlade-Chamberlain had proved effective when chipping in with some vital goals but unfortunately suffered a serious injury in the semi-final first leg against AS Roma.

If there was any area for concern, it centred around the goalkeeper position, where Loris Karius had dislodged Simon Mignolet, but for the second year running the goals against column had improved. Although Liverpool exited both domestic cup competitions early, their form in the Premier League was again impressive and a 4-0 victory at home to Brighton & Hove Albion on the final day saw them secure a top four finish for the second successive season.

It was in the Champions League though that Klopp's team really captured the attention. The impressive fashion in which they had emerged unscathed from the group phase before swatting aside Porto, Manchester City and Roma highlighted the fine job the manager was doing.

He had now guided Liverpool to their third cup final appearance in three years, a notable return but one that was yet to yield the most precious commodity.

"I see no trophies after these games," mused Klopp in the build-up to the 2018 Champions League Final. "They don't hang silver medals at Melwood. There is still a job to do." But as he was to discover once again at Kyiv's Olympiyskiy Stadium, that last step to success is often the toughest.

Any team other than serial Kings of Europe Real Madrid would have feared a one-off showdown with Liverpool but the odds were stacked in favour of the Spanish giants, who were aiming for a third successive continental crown and their 13th win in total.

Klopp firmly believed his team had a chance, though, and was quick to remind everyone why: "We are Liverpool." It was as simple as that.

Infused with the belief of their manager, Liverpudlians made the arduous trek to the Ukrainian capital in their thousands, ready to party and make new memories on the banks of the Dnieper. They danced the day away in Shevchenko Park, where red flags and banners hung from trees, then sang along with Dua Lipa inside the stadium prior to kick-off.

On the pitch, despite the underdog tag, Liverpool were confident and they started strong, only for it to quickly unravel around the half-hour mark when a stricken Mo Salah was forced to leave the field in tears, clutching an injured shoulder after a challenge by Sergio Ramos.

"A big moment in the game," was Klopp's diplomatic assessment of the incident, which was to have a detrimental effect on the ultimate outcome. Having lost their main goal threat in such controversial circumstances, Liverpool's early

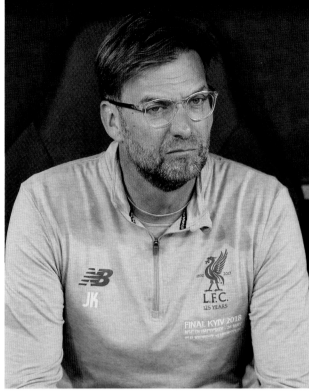

optimism began to drain. It got worse when a goalkeeping error by Loris Karius gifted Zinedine Zidane's side the opening goal.

To their credit, Liverpool bounced back, but only briefly. Sadio Mané drew them level four minutes later, before a stunning overhead kick by substitute Gareth Bale reclaimed the advantage. Another mistake by Karius then provided Bale with his second goal of the night to confirm a defeat that was both gut-wrenching and heart-breaking. Red shirts slumped to the floor and more tears flowed. "It was not the best script for us tonight," said a despondent Klopp in his post-match press conference. "We wanted everything and got nothing."

It was a desperately disappointing way to end what had been such a positive season and the manner of defeat made it an even more bitter pill to swallow. Klopp's cup final curse had struck again.

By the early hours of the following morning, spirits were slowly beginning to lift. A video of the manager singing went viral and it sent out a defiant message that there was always next year…

"We saw the European Cup,
Madrid had all the f**king luck,
We swear, we keep on being cool,
We bring it back to Liverpool."

"Three hours before the Champions League Final in Kyiv was the final team meeting and I think he could sense we were a little bit anxious or nervous. He started the meeting showing his underpants that were CR7 ones, so Cristiano Ronaldo No.7. He said, 'I didn't do it on purpose because my wife packs my underwear and socks. These were the only pants left.' That was the beginning of the meeting before the Champions League Final, so that took a lot of pressure off the team. He changed how I saw football. The famous Jürgen Klopp tactic 'gegenpressing', it doesn't work with only one detail, it's a whole system. He could explain it really well and everybody understood what they needed to do. He's able to take those complicated things and make them simple. This is where he's really good. He changed me as a footballer and a human being."

RAGNAR KLAVAN

NEVER
GIVE UP

2018–19

ALLEZ, ALLEZ, ALLEZ

Pre-season tour, July 2018

Despite losing the Champions League Final, there remained a feel-good factor around Liverpool in the summer of 2018. The resurgence under Jürgen Klopp even had its own soundtrack and it continued to buzz in the ears of everyone.

'Allez, Allez, Allez' had first surfaced prior to the round of 16 tie in Porto and quickly caught on, echoing around Europe during the remainder of the team's exciting run to Kyiv. Based on a 1980s dance tune by Italian duo Righeira, the lyrics had been re-written by Liverpudlians Phil Howard and Liam Malone. It celebrated the club's past European exploits but was very much a song for the moment.

One of the many thousands of supporters who had been trekking across the continent to support the Reds during this time was the then 24-year-old electrician and part-time musician Jamie Webster. To him and many likeminded others, Klopp was the new messiah, and it was thanks to him that they were living their best lives watching Liverpool.

Webster was becoming well-known among the club's local fanbase for performing in the pubs around Anfield on matchdays, especially gaining a reputation with those who regularly attended the popular post-match Boss Night sessions in Liverpool city centre.

The abiding memory of Kyiv for most travelling fans had been the pre-match party in Shevchenko Park. At the heart of that was Webster, belting out the club's unofficial new anthem. As his fame began to spread, he was invited by the club to perform for US-based supporters during the pre-season tour that summer.

Klopp had long bought into the unique fan culture that surrounded Liverpool, of which Webster was now a central part. He admitted to loving this song and being a big fan of the singer. "I like Jamie without knowing him because I've seen a few videos of him singing. It's really nice how he lives that song!"

When an opportunity arose during this tour to meet him, the boss didn't hesitate and decided to make a surprise visit to one of the Stateside gigs in Michigan. A shell-shocked Webster was stopped in his tracks mid-performance and, for once, left speechless before launching into another rousing rendition of 'Allez, Allez, Allez'.

"With Jamie, it was quite an easy decision that I would go in," revealed Klopp. "I had no clue what was behind the door, how many people or whatever – I had never been in that room before." The manager promptly joined in, displaying the

"It was the first time I'd ever met Jürgen and it was a moment I'll never forget. After he came in to watch me sing at the gig, we spent about five minutes together just talking about footy and music. I couldn't believe it; this was the manager of the club I love taking time out to show a genuine interest in me, just a young match-going Scouse lad. The video of him surprising me then went viral and it really kick-started my career as a musician. I've said it before, but Jürgen Klopp really is a better human being than he is a football manager — and that's saying something in itself, because I think he's the best football manager in the world. I'll never be able to repay him for what he's done for me. As fans we owe him everything, and he owes us nothing. Forever Jürgen."

JAMIE WEBSTER

same enthusiasm he shows on the touchline, singing every word and mirroring the actions of the watching crowd.

It was an impromptu but heart-warming moment. The manager recognised that football is all about enjoying the journey and that songs like this play a massive part in that. "If we all move in the right direction, the fans, players and staff, it's not a guarantee, but a formula that means success is more likely," Klopp told Webster.

Here was a true man of the people. A manager in tune with his supporters. Together they would make Liverpool stronger.

PITCH INVADER

Liverpool v Everton | Premier League, 2 December 2018

Feelings in football arguably don't come much better than last-minute winners or victories against your local rivals. Under Jürgen Klopp both had become a common occurrence at Liverpool. Combine the two and, as Klopp would say, "Boom!"

Almost two years had elapsed since the Sadio Mané derby at Goodison Park. Two years can be a long time in football but, on Merseyside, you're not allowed to forget what's gone before. Liverpudlians were still singing about it and Evertonians were still smarting over it.

For the first time since Klopp took over, Liverpool were also now mounting a serious title challenge and breathing down the neck of league leaders Manchester City, winning 10 and drawing three of their opening 13 games. So, on this occasion, there was slightly more than local pride at stake. This was represented in the added intensity of the battle. Both sides did their best to cancel each other out and chances were spurned at either end.

As the closing stages loomed, the match remained goalless, then, in the 86th minute, Klopp played what proved to be his trump card, sending on forgotten forward Divock Origi in place of Roberto Firmino. It was a substitution that would hardly have set alarms bells ringing in the opposition dugout. Origi had played just

Below and next page:
Jordan Pickford is helpless to prevent Divock Origi heading home a sensational late winner.

"With his personality and vision, the impact
Jürgen had at this club, and his influence on
me, was unbelievable. He was a father figure
who managed me from when I was young
and helped me grow so much, on and off the
pitch. He knew how to get the best out of me
and always showed the utmost faith in me.
This gave me all the confidence I needed
whenever I went out onto the pitch. 'Just
go out and play your game,' he said when
sending me on against Everton. It was a
high-pressure match, but he knew what
I could do. The goal was like a movie scene,
it couldn't have been scripted any better.
We enjoyed so many memorable moments
like this. He was a such special manager and,
alongside the likes of Shankly, Dalglish and
Gerrard, a huge pillar in Liverpool's history."

DIVOCK ORIGI

11 minutes of first-team football all season and hadn't appeared in the Premier League since the opening day of the previous campaign but, as the manager explained, "Our idea was clear. We wanted to win until the last second and we wanted to show that by bringing strikers on."

As the match entered stoppage time, the visitors looked to have settled for the draw, content in the knowledge that they'd played well and were not going to be beaten. Klopp had other ideas.

Amid whistles and jeers from the away end, and one last almighty roar from the Kop, a forward pass from Trent Alexander-Arnold was headed clear but only to Virgil van Dijk, who swung a foot at it from the edge of the box, sending the ball skywards towards the Everton goal.

Supporters started turning towards the exits until the keeper somehow failed to deal with it, pushing the ball onto the bar and subsequently the head of an inrushing Origi. From point blank range, the Belgian nodded the ball over the line, sparking madness and mayhem.

On the sidelines Klopp lost all control and raced 40 yards across the pitch, where he jumped into the arms of Alisson Becker before storming back to embrace his assistant Pep Lijnders. "The goal was lucky of course," he reflected, "but it was a long and open game and I think we deserved the points."

Origi's goal will forever be part of Anfield folklore. Klopp later apologised for any offence his overexuberance may have caused but, given the circumstances, he could hardly be blamed.

SAVE OF THE SEASON

Liverpool v Napoli | Champions League Group Phase, 11 December 2018

In December 2018, Liverpool's Champions League aspirations hung in the balance. It was matchday six and the final round of group fixtures. In contrast to the previous season, when they had coasted through this phase unbeaten, three away defeats this term had condemned them to a nerve-wracking do-or-die drama.

After exceeding expectations and going all the way to the final a season before, this time around they had flattered to deceive in the competition and now ran the risk of dropping down to the Europa League. For Jürgen Klopp, it was a nightmare scenario that he dared not contemplate.

Having strengthened again in the summer, this Liverpool team was, in his eyes, as close to the finished article as it had ever been.

The most significant signing had been that of the highly rated Roma goalkeeper Alisson Becker. In light of the errors that blighted the final in Kyiv, Klopp had immediately prioritised the search for a new number one and didn't hesitate in making Alisson the most expensive keeper on the planet. Described by one of his former coaches at Roma as "the Messi of goalkeepers" because he could "define an era", the fact he conceded five at Anfield in May had no impact whatsoever on the manager's judgement.

"When the opportunity came up to sign one of the world's best goalkeepers, then it's not a long thought," explained Klopp. "I think it's something we have to do. He has nothing to do with the price, we have nothing to do with the price, it's the market, that's how it is and we will not think a lot about it. It shows the value of goalkeepers, of course, in this moment."

Other new faces included midfielders Fabinho from Monaco and Naby Keita from RB Leipzig, plus the more attack-minded Xherdan Shaqiri from Stoke City. But it was the Brazilian stopper who had been the missing link. He was the final piece in the jigsaw for Klopp, the all-important base of the team's spine. Nights and situations like this were exactly what big players such as Alisson had been bought for.

Liverpool, third in the group at the start of play, had to win with a clean sheet or by two clear goals to secure qualification. They should never have been in the position they now found themselves in when it came to the Champions League, but Klopp remained hopeful. "We have a chance, and we will give everything to try and use it," he confidently stated ahead of the game. Opponents Napoli, managed by Carlo Ancelotti, sat second behind leaders Paris Saint-Germain, while even

bottom-placed club Red Star Belgrade were still in with a chance of progressing. It was far from straightforward, but another sizzling occasion awaited, one that required cool heads and safe hands.

It would also need the prolific golden boot of Mo Salah and it was the Egyptian King who scored the all-important goal in the 34th minute, using his skill to cut inside and beat the keeper at the near post. "What a goal, unbelievable," said Klopp but that told only half the story of an extremely anxious night. "The most difficult period was directly after the 1-0," he added. "You could see this little bit of relief and then immediately Napoli were there. That made the game so intense."

While one-nil was enough to send Liverpool through, more goals would have eased the rising tension around Anfield. If even one goal was conceded, they could have been heading out. It was difficult to know whether they should stick or twist. Liverpool tried in vain to score another and as time wore on the threat of Napoli snatching it increased.

Alisson had experienced busier nights, but concentration was key. When called upon, he showed exactly why Klopp had been prepared to spend so much on him. In the third minute of injury time, he came to the rescue with what remains, perhaps, his most famous save, a stunning close-range stop to deny Arkadiusz Milik.

Unmarked and with the ball at his feet in the six-yard box, the Napoli substitute couldn't have wished for a more clear-cut opportunity. Time seemingly stood still

"The way Jürgen spoke to the coaching staff at our first meeting, it felt like he had known us all for years. His man-management skills were second to none and his positivity shone through. He got everyone fully behind the team again and instilled a belief that we could become a winning force. Although he had the final say on everything, he encouraged staff to have a say. He always listened to what I said and trusted my opinion. I had been following Ali's progress since 2013 so knew how good he was. We regularly worked on replicating match situations in training but it's difficult to prepare for what happened against Napoli. That save proved to be a massive moment in our season and for everything that followed but all credit goes to Jürgen. We've all benefited from working with him and, for what he achieved here, he deserves a statue."

JOHN ACHTERBERG

and hearts missed a beat as he lined up his shot but Alisson was out in a flash to open his body up and make the crucial block.

If the ball had gone in, Liverpool's journey to Madrid would have been over in an instant, and afterwards Klopp was purring with understandable pride. "Wow, what a game. I am not sure a manager could be prouder of a team than I am. It was wild and there were lots of counterattacks, but we were ready for that."

The highest praise though was, not surprisingly, reserved for his keeper. "I have no idea how he makes a save like this. I have no words for it. That was the lifesaver tonight. If I knew Alisson was this good, I would have paid double for him."

Alisson had not only secured Liverpool's place in the knockout phase of the competition for the second successive season and kept the club on course for a potential number six, he'd also bucked a trend in terms of Anfield's previous European heroes. It's a list dominated by the names of those who had scored the vital goals. On this occasion it was the turn of a goalkeeper to take the plaudits, and deservedly so.

The importance of a solid spine had never been better illustrated, and Jürgen Klopp's decision to invest in Alisson Becker had been vindicated. Liverpool's season was starting to get interesting again.

BEATING BAYERN

Bayern Munich v Liverpool | Champions League round of 16 2nd leg, 13 March 2019

Jürgen Klopp was a man on a mission. Having got so close to the Champions League trophy in 2017/18, he was determined to go one better this year. But if he was to keep Liverpool on track, he first he had to exorcise some demons from his past.

The spectre of Bayern Munich was one that had haunted him ever since his Borussia Dortmund side had been beaten by them in the final at Wembley six years before and they now stood in the way of him making further progress in this season's competition. If he were able to defeat his old nemesis on the way to the final, it would render making it there all the more sweeter.

Domestically, Liverpool were slugging it out with Manchester City at the top of the Premier League table, and it was whispered that Europe could be a distraction from their title ambitions. A narrow defeat away to City in early January remained their only Premier League loss, and there was genuine belief that this could be the year they finally ended their long wait for that crown.

Above:
The home fans inside Munich's Allianz Arena are silenced by one of Liverpool's great European performances.

"To come up against Jürgen's Liverpool as a Bayern player in the 2018/19 Champions League was amazing but at the time, they were too strong. We were not in our best condition, and it was difficult, a tough defeat to take. It has since been a great, life-changing experience for me to play under him at Liverpool, where I learned to play a different type of game to what I'd previously been used to. Being comfortable in the middle of chaos was one of his goals in our team during games. Creating this high-intensity football, causing trouble for the opposition and exposing their weaknesses. It takes time to understand that and to adapt your in-game decisions in these high-speed situations, but Jürgen helped me adapt and evolve. I am thankful to him for giving me the opportunity to be part of this city, this club and this community."

THIAGO ALCANTARA

Equally, there were high hopes of Liverpool conquering Europe for a sixth time. The boss headed back to his homeland for the second leg, insisting success on both fronts was well within their capabilities.

Following a dour and frustrating goalless draw in the first meeting at Anfield, it was Bayern who held the upper hand. Klopp's task in Munich was made even more difficult when his captain Jordan Henderson limped off with an injury after just 13 minutes at the Allianz Arena.

However, it proved to be one of those pivotal moments that can so often galvanise a team. Midway through the half, Sadio Mané gave Liverpool the lead with a spectacular goal that was so special, Klopp admitted he "would watch it a thousand times".

It put Liverpool firmly in the driving seat. Parity was restored when Joel Matip unfortunately turned the ball into his own net just before half-time, but the manager remained calm. "In a game like this there will be mistakes, but you have to stay in the game and try and control it in the moments you can control it."

After the break Liverpool regained control, stifling Bayern's star-studded attack and eventually putting the outcome beyond any doubt with two more goals, courtesy of Virgil van Dijk and Mané again. "In the moments we did play football we immediately destroyed the organisation of Bayern. It's absolutely deserved," enthused Klopp.

A night that began nervously ended comfortably; Liverpool had been that good. It was a European masterclass by Klopp's side and one of the club's best-ever results on foreign soil. "We've laid down a marker tonight that LFC is back on the top level of European football," he proudly boasted.

For Jürgen Klopp, victory here meant everything. The pain inflicted on him by Bayern had finally been eased and Liverpool had taken a major step closer towards the banishing their own Champions League demons.

Above left:
Jürgen's smile says it all after overseeing a momentous victory back in his homeland.

Above right:
Virgil van Dijk rises highest to restore Liverpool's lead.

CORNER TAKEN QUICKLY

Liverpool v Barcelona | Champions League semi-final 2nd leg, 7 May 2019

It was deemed the impossible task. A step too far even for Jürgen Klopp and the incredible Liverpool team he had assembled. Long before a ball had been kicked in this semi-final second leg, Liverpool's chances of overturning a three goal deficit at home to Barcelona had been written off by almost everyone.

After what had been yet another thrilling run in the competition, it was tough for fans to accept. But little did they know, in the away team changing room following defeat at the Nou Camp, the first seeds were being sown for a comeback that would go down in history as one of the greatest of all time.

Liverpool had played well enough in the first leg only to be undone by the brilliance of Lionel Messi and Luis Suarez. Klopp accepted the odds were now heavily stacked against them, but he and his coaches made sure heads didn't drop. He ordered his players to believe, repeating the word over and over again. "Nothing is lost," he told them. "I believe. As long as there are chances, I believe. We will turn this around."

Never before had a Liverpool team fought back from such an emphatic first leg defeat, although the Champions League Final of 2005 was proof that miracles can happen, and Barcelona had also squandered a similar lead against Roma as recently as the previous season. At his pre-match press conference, Klopp spoke confidently. "Yes, there's hope. We are far from giving up," he insisted. "But we are not in a situation where we say, 'It will happen, 100 per cent'. It's football and that's why we give it a try because of the boys and the character of the boys."

The challenge they faced was made worse when Mo Salah and Roberto Firmino were both ruled out through injury. Supporters were still reeling from that news when they heard that Manchester City had defeated Leicester to edge ahead in the title race with just one game remaining. A season that promised so much was in danger of falling flat.

Despite all this, Klopp was keen to ensure that the mood remained as upbeat as it could. He didn't want the supporters turning up at Anfield feeling sorry for themselves and urged everyone to make it an occasion to remember. "It should be a football party. We don't drink during the game – no alcohol at least – so we should then celebrate it with football. That's the plan.

"It's possible and a little bit likely that it will be the last Champions League game for this campaign, so let's celebrate it with our legs, with our lungs, with good decisions, with a sensational atmosphere and all that stuff. Then we will see

Opposite: Two Gini Wijnaldum goals in quick succession helped turn the tie in Liverpool's favour.

what's the outcome. If we can do it, wonderful. If we can't do it, let's fail in the most beautiful way."

It was an act of genius, and he reserved some special words for the players too. On the afternoon of the match, at the city centre hotel where he had signed the contract to become Liverpool manager in 2015, Klopp called everyone together for the usual pre-match team meeting. He glanced around the room to check everyone was present then began...

"What we do tonight, I would say, is impossible. If it was any other group of players in the world 3-0 down to Barcelona after the first leg, I'd say we've got no chance. I'd say play for pride, play for dignity. I'd say go out with your heads held high. But this is not any other group of players. Because it's you, there is a chance." It was Shankly-esque in its delivery and will be remembered as one of the most significant pre-match team talks in the club's history.

Hours later and with those words of inspiration still ringing in their ears, a depleted Liverpool side walked out at a raucous Anfield. The sense of belief Klopp had instilled in his players had also infused the fans and a renewed air of hope radiated from the stands. The injured Salah looked on from the sidelines sporting a black t-shirt with 'Never Give Up' emblazoned across the front. It encapsulated the mood perfectly.

The game couldn't have started any better for Liverpool. Within seven minutes Divock Origi, starting only in the absence of Firmino, lit the blue touch paper when

he swept the ball home from close-range to startle the visitors. Klopp's celebration was a restrained one: he turned to Main Stand, fists clenched low but with a knowing look on his face. For anyone who thought this comeback was beyond his team, it was suddenly a case of 'think again'.

The early breakthrough was crucial, and it lifted the spirits of everyone that little bit more. The crowd had already pledged their unconditional support for the team, but this opening goal spurred them on to roar even louder.

There was to be no further scoring in a first half that saw Andy Robertson added to the manager's growing list of injury problems but during the break Klopp reiterated the magic word "believe" and re-emphasised the need for patience, reminding his players that didn't matter when the goals came, as long they did come.

Perhaps Robertson's withdrawal was fate because his replacement, Georginio Wijnaldum, was to have major impact. Just nine minutes into the second period the Dutch midfielder slammed in a low cross from the right to reduce the deficit further. The decibels rose, belief soared and Barca were getting twitchy.

Two minutes later Wijnaldum did it again and the roof was almost blown off the Kop. This time the cross came in from the left and he outjumped the defence to send a powerful twisting header into the top corner. Now we were in the realms of the unthinkable and there was still over half an hour to go.

The night wasn't without its heart-stopping moments at the opposite end though. A goal for Barca would change everything and Alisson, in a one-off light grey strip, was once again in "world-class" form to keep their star-studded attack at bay.

At the start of the night every Liverpudlian would have given their right arm for the game to go to extra time or penalties but now it was the Spaniards who were praying for the full-time whistle and some much-needed pain relief from the cosh they were under. Eleven minutes remained and Liverpool had the bit between their teeth.

Then they won a corner on the right. Trent Alexander-Arnold took it quickly, picking out an unmarked Origi. What happened next is the stuff of legend. An unsuspecting defence had switched off and Origi swept the ball home from close range to complete the most miraculous of comebacks.

Klopp hailed the goal as "incredibly smart," but confessed he had no idea who took the corner or who scored because it had happened so fast.

Scenes of sheer pandemonium broke out all around the ground and, overcome with emotion, Klopp completely lost himself in the moment. Speaking to one of the on-pitch television reporters immediately after the final whistle, he didn't hold back. "These boys are f**king giants," he roared. "The whole performance, the whole game was actually too much, it was overwhelming. You play against maybe

Next page:
The comeback begins as Divock Origi scores from close range to give Liverpool a 1-0 lead.

"The greatest gift Jürgen gave to Liverpool was belief. He united the entire club – the players, the staff, the fans – and instilled a spirit whereby if we all pulled together in the same direction, anything was possible. This was never better illustrated than against Barcelona in the Champions League semi-final. No-one gave us a chance of coming back from three goals down, apart from him, and what he did so well was transmit those positive thoughts to the players. The way he delivered his speech at our pre-match meeting was amazing. It made us all feel ten feet tall, and we walked out of that room with a renewed sense of optimism. He made us believe that miracles can happen and that this team was more than capable of overturning the deficit. What he said to us that day will live with me forever."

JORDAN HENDERSON

the best team in the world, you're not allowed to concede, you have to score… I don't know how we did it. I don't know how the boys did it, it was incredible.

"It's a special night, very special. Winning against Barcelona is obviously one of the most difficult things in the world of football. We know this club is the mix of atmosphere, emotion, desire and football quality. Cut off one and it doesn't work – we know that. I've said it before. If I have to describe this club then it's a big heart and tonight it was obviously pounding like crazy. You could hear it and probably feel it all over the world."

Even the most seasoned of observers couldn't believe what they had just witnessed. Anfield, with its rich history of epic European escapades under the lights, had a wonderfully heroic new story, one that people will never tire of telling. "I've watched in my life so many football games, I can't remember a lot like this. I will remember it forever," said Klopp. He wasn't alone.

A lasting image of the euphoric aftermath is of the manager, together with his players and entire backroom staff, stood in unison, singing and swaying as 'You'll Never Walk Alone' blasted out from the Kop. It was reminiscent of that afternoon against West Brom back in 2015 but the team had come a long way since then.

When the dust settled and celebrations finally subsided, the realisation sank in that Klopp now had a second successive Champions League Final to prepare for. "I'm so happy we could give the people this experience and I'm really happy about having another chance to get things right from our point of view."

Led by Jürgen Klopp, Liverpool had proved that anything is possible.

KINGS OF EUROPE

Liverpool v Tottenham Hotspur | Champions League Final, 1 June 2019

Jürgen Klopp and his players stood tantalisingly on the cusp of greatness, immortality even. Those who have the honour of being a European Champion are destined to be feted forever and Liverpool were now just 90 minutes away from the ultimate prize.

Klopp, of course, had been here twice before, in 2013 with Dortmund and 2018 with Liverpool, only to twice fall back into the abyss. The pressure to succeed this time was enormous. The 2019 Champions League Final was his fourth cup final as Liverpool manager, and he was yet to win one.

There were plausible reasons as to why the Reds didn't see the job through on the previous occasions. With each of those losses came the caveat that they were part of a learning curve, and that brighter times lay ahead.

This time there would be no hiding place for failure. After four years with Klopp at the helm, it was time for Liverpool Football Club to rejoin the trophy-winning ranks. Klopp was aware of this as much as anyone. "I could write a book about winning semi-finals, but no-one would buy it," he joked. "I get it that we have to win things. It's really important for us that people don't ask all the time about this. It's also important for our development as a team."

Having been pipped at the post by just a single point in the Premier League title race, Liverpool's season now rested on this game. There are only so many disappointments a team can take. Defeat here was unthinkable.

Aiming to inflict more misery on them were familiar foes from North London, Tottenham Hotspur, who themselves had been involved in a dramatic semi-final, against Ajax. It was the first time Liverpool had contested an all-English European final, but it didn't detract from the excitement or sense of occasion.

It had been 14 years since the trophy known affectionately around Anfield as 'old big ears' had been etched with the initials LFC. It was too long for the five-time Kings of Europe. Klopp's ambition was to follow in the footsteps of Bob Paisley (1977, 1978, 1981), Joe Fagan (1984) and Rafael Benitez (2005).

The Estadio Metropolitano in Madrid was the venue for this much longed-for day of destiny and the Spanish capital was swamped by a sea of red, a Scouse armada that had sailed into the city intent on having the best of times and savouring what everyone hoped would be a historic occasion.

In the three weeks that had separated the end of the domestic season and the Champions League Final, Klopp had given the players some much-needed time off.

He then took them to Marbella for a week-long training camp to switch off from the many demands brought on in the build-up to games of such magnitude and get them acclimatised to the searing heat that would greet them in Madrid.

Five more days of preparation back at Melwood completed a programme that had been meticulously planned, and the first day of June couldn't come soon enough. Klopp and his team were ready. This was it. The biggest game of their lives.

The early evening sun had not yet dipped behind the stands and some supporters were still finding their seats when the 2019 Champions League Final exploded into life. A cagey affair between two sides that knew each other so well had been predicted but after just 22 seconds of the first ball being played there was drama. Sadio Mané's attempted cross was adjudged to have been handled just inside the box by Moussa Sissoko and the Slovenian referee pointed immediately to the spot.

Debate raged as to whether it was the right decision or not. Tottenham players protested and it went to a VAR check. The delay heightened the mounting tension. It's just as well Liverpool's designated penalty taker Mo Salah had ice running through his veins. Unperturbed, he stepped up a minute later and with his wand of a left foot confidently drove his kick past the despairing dive of Hugo Lloris.

It had been the most dramatic start to a Champions League Final since AC Milan had raced into an early lead against Liverpool in 2005, but a similar thrilling spectacle failed to materialise. Although Tottenham had plenty of time to respond,

"My experience of the Champions League Final is, of course, not great, but it was a joy to play against Jürgen and his team, in a tactical way and how he is on the touchline. It was always a good challenge to be there and … when you share the space, next to him you feel he's a special guy. We compete to win but in the end you must also have big respect for the opponent. Sometimes when you win it's not easy to keep quiet and be respectful of the opponent but, as always, he showed great respect and that is a thing I appreciate a lot. He's a great man. A great coach. A great person. Always in my mind he's a manager that translates his character to the team. He was building the first few years, then started to play finals and challenge for big trophies. What he created at Liverpool is amazing."

MAURICIO POCHETTINO

Above: The left foot of Divock Origi seals victory against Spurs and the club's sixth European Cup.

Next page: Campione Liverpool! Jürgen gets his hands on the most coveted prize in European club football.

their initial gameplan went out of the window, which suited Liverpool. Klopp instructed his players to just concentrate and stay focused. The onus was on their opponents to come out and attack. It was all about game management. In the words of the manager, "no risks, no chance for mistakes".

Goalscoring opportunities were few and far between at both ends but without the 'golden gloves' of Alisson the balance could have swung a few times. With such a slender lead, everyone was starting to get nervous. As the night wore on, though, Tottenham became more frustrated by the minute and began to tire.

Liverpool seemed to have more energy and eventually, with just four minutes remaining, they made it tell. Joel Matip was the unlikely provider, feeding substitute Divock Origi inside the opposition box. Origi, hero of the semi-final, took one touch with his right boot then unleashed a shot with his left that rolled low into the bottom far corner of the net.

The Liverpudlians directly behind that goal were in ecstasy. Liverpool Football Club had conquered Europe for a sixth time, taken back to the promised land by Jürgen Norbert Klopp.

While bedlam broke out all around him, the manager's immediate reaction when the final whistle blew was to throw a consoling arm around his opposite number Mauricio Pochettino. "I know how Tottenham feel in this moment better than anybody else in the world. They played a sensational season as well, but tonight we scored the goals in the right moment," he later explained.

Klopp then looked up to the stands, where he picked out his family and friends, waved and blew them a kiss. Consumed by overwhelming happiness and sheer relief, it was difficult to contain his emotions. "Did you ever see a team like this? I am so happy for the boys, all these people and my family. They suffer for me, they deserve it more than anybody. The final is about the result and tonight the boys showed the resilience we needed. I don't want to explain why we won it; I only want to enjoy that we won it."

As Jordan Henderson went up to lift the cup, Klopp declined an invitation from his skipper to join him on the presentation podium and watched on proudly, almost out of sight. To him, this was a moment for the players, and he was more than happy for them to take centre stage. "It wasn't important for me to touch the cup. I loved seeing the boys having it and seeing some faces in the crowd. That is what gave me everything I need."

In appreciation of their efforts, he went around each and every one of them, dishing out his now trademark 'Klopp hugs'. "The players were all pretty much crying on the pitch because it was so emotional, it was so big, it means so much to us," said Klopp. Those same players recognised that without the manager it would not have been possible, and they returned the compliment by tossing him into the air and carrying him victoriously towards the Liverpool fans, who were desperate to pay homage to him themselves.

Klopp's promise to deliver a title within four years had been fulfilled. It had been the culmination of so much blood, sweat and tears, but to eventually get his hands on that most magnificent trophy made it all worthwhile. "It was an intense season with the most beautiful finish I ever could have imagined. It is the best night of our professional lives," he reflected.

The party of all parties was only just starting, and Klopp turned up to his post-match press conference clutching a celebratory beer. "It's for all the people around the world, in the stadium. They are with us and now celebrating like crazy," he said. "We'll celebrate together, we'll have a sensational night."

For Liverpool, as a club, and for Klopp, personally, it was such a momentous occasion. Seven years had passed since both had last won a trophy. Now, after four years, they had achieved success together for the first time and the boss was predicting an even brighter future. "For me, I'm really happy. I have a lot of silver medals and now I have a golden one. And now we won something, we will carry on. We want to win things, 100 per cent. This is only the start."

In winning number six, Liverpool had also moved into the realms of European royalty. Only two clubs had won this most coveted piece of silver more times and for the role they played in achieving this, Jürgen Klopp and his players had fully earned the legendary status that comes with it.

ALL ABOARD THE MAGIC BUS

Homecoming Parade, 2 June 2019

Liverpool is a city renowned for its party vibe and Scousers certainly know how to have a good time, but the Liver Birds had not witnessed a celebration on this scale since the Champions League trophy had last come home to roost on the banks of the red and white Mersey in 2005.

From the moment Divock Origi's goal hit the back of the net in Madrid, Liverpudlians everywhere had been in a state of euphoria. Nobody slept much, including Klopp. In the immediate aftermath of the match at the Metropolitano, the manager admitted he couldn't wait for the following day's victory parade. "Going to Liverpool tomorrow with something to celebrate is big and I'm really looking forward to that."

Bleary-eyed, hoarse and still emotional from the wild night before, Liverpool's victorious squad touched down at John Lennon Airport early Sunday afternoon,

their plane greeted on the tarmac by a ceremonial water arc, which is a salute traditionally reserved only for visiting foreign dignitaries or military veterans.

As the bus, draped in red and emblazoned with those three magical words 'CHAMPIONS OF EUROPE', set off on its journey, the rising excitement in the city reached fever pitch.

Supporters had been lining the streets since early in the morning, determined to secure the best vantage point. From its starting point in Allerton, it was to be a slow but glorious meandering crawl through the suburbs of Childwall, Broadgreen, West Derby, Tuebrook and Kensington, towards its final city centre destination.

The pavements were a thronging mass of red. Klopp and his players took turns to show off the trophy that shimmered like a diamond as supporters desperately clambered onto rooftops, bus stops and traffic lights to catch a glimpse.

At various points, Klopp could be spotted at the back of the bus enjoying a moment to himself; legs dangling over the side, beer in hand and baseball cap turned backwards, just soaking it all up. The sights were a joy to behold and the manager was completely taken aback by what he was witnessing. "It's really

Opposite:
An estimated 750,000 people turned out to salute the 2019 Champions of Europe.

Above:
The jubilant Liverpool players bask in the glory of their Champions League success.

special. You see in their eyes how much it means. It's unbelievable and it's so intense. Today, wow! It's crazy."

The crowds were at their most dense along the city's iconic waterfront. Liver Birds looked proudly down on the epic scenes as clouds of red smoke filled the air, tickertape floated down and fireworks exploded.

It was a truly breath-taking reception, one befitting the new Kings of Europe. Klopp was almost lost for words. "I cannot really describe it. I cried a little bit because it's so overwhelming what the people are doing. It's brilliant."

It was estimated that three quarters of a million people had turned out to hail the 2019 Champions League winners, making it the biggest homecoming in the city's history – one that eclipsed even that of The Beatles when they returned home from the United States back in the 60s.

Jürgen Klopp was creating something special here and if proof was ever needed, this was it.

"When he arrived, he promised to turn doubters into believers. He certainly did that and then some. We are a club that adores the managers that have brought us happiness and victories over the decades, and we recognise them with flags and banners on the Kop. A hundred years from now, there will be Jürgen Klopp banners flying proudly, if not an even more permanent recognition of the indelible mark he left on this club, and its fans, both locally here on Merseyside and globally in every corner of this planet. For me, I will never forget being with him on the bus the day after winning the Champions League in 2019. As we passed through the streets of Liverpool, grown men were sobbing as he proudly showed them the trophy. At that moment, perhaps more than any other manager in our history, he was one of us. I'm so glad Jürgen was a Red."

PETER MOORE FORMER LIVERPOOL FC
CHIEF EXECUTIVE OFFICER

BOOM! ENDING THE 30-YEAR WAIT

2019–20

SUPER REDS

Liverpool v Chelsea, UEFA Super Cup Final, 14 August 2019

At a club that exists to win trophies, any opportunity to collect more silverware has to be treated seriously. Fortunately, Jürgen Klopp was of this exact opinion and his thirst for success was becoming an insatiable one.

As European champions, Liverpool had qualified for the UEFA Super Cup, which took them to Istanbul in the opening weeks of the 2019/20 campaign.

It was another all-English affair against a club Klopp would become very familiar with when it came to contesting cup finals. A few weeks before Liverpool defeated Tottenham to claim the Champions League, Chelsea had beaten Arsenal to clinch the Europa League.

Turkey seemed like a long way to travel so soon into the season for what some label as nothing more than a glorified friendly or a continental version of the Community Shield. But with another trophy on offer, one Liverpool had won three times in the past, there was never a chance this would be taken lightly.

No German coach had won the Super Cup before. Klopp admitted to originally not being fully aware of how important it was, but the fact it was listed on the Champions Wall at the club's training ground was enough to convince him.

Below: Another season, another trophy, this time the UEFA Super Cup.

The team he selected was as strong as it could be, aside from one position change that had been forced on him. During the Premier League opener five days

earlier, Alisson Becker had suffered an injury that ruled him out of this trip. His place went to Adrian, a keeper who had been without a club two weeks previously. Signed on a free transfer as goalkeeping cover, his chance came a lot sooner than expected and he fully grasped it.

In what was a full-blooded encounter at Besiktas Park, Sadio Mané scored twice for the Reds, but not even extra time could separate the two teams and a 2-2 draw meant penalties. It was via a shoot-out in this city that Liverpool had, of course, famously won the Champions League in 2005. Jerzy Dudek was the goalkeeping hero back then and this time it would be Adrian who saved the decisive kick to win the cup for Liverpool.

"He put in an incredible performance," said Klopp afterwards. "It was all about winning, and we did that in the end. It was a big fight tonight and I didn't know before the game how good it would be when you win it, but it's brilliant, it's really big. It's not about me winning it, it's about LFC winning it, winning it for all the people who support us, and I can feel how much it meant to all these people and that makes me really happy."

Like waiting for a bus, it had taken a while for Jürgen Klopp's first trophy as Liverpool manager but two had now come along in quick succession. The taste of champagne was one he and his players were getting used to.

Above: Jürgen and members of his backroom team enjoying the Super Cup success in Istanbul.

Next page: Adrian San Miguel, on his full debut for the club, emerged the hero against Chelsea.

"This game capped a crazy week for me, and it came just days after arriving. The boss said he signed me because of my experience and personality, and this gave me all the confidence I needed. Saving that penalty to win the cup is a great memory. It couldn't have been scripted any better. It was a dream come true and I will always be grateful to him for showing faith in me. He helped change my mentality and I quickly found that his footballing philosophy just fitted in so well with all of the players. It's because of this that he was able to build brilliant teams. There isn't any real secret to the success he's had other than that. He really is so normal, so human, but 100 per cent he will be remembered forever as a great manager, not just in Liverpool but throughout the world."

ADRIAN SAN MIGUEL

NEVER SAY DIE

Aston Villa v Liverpool | Premier League, 2 November 2019

An unwanted anniversary was fast approaching at Anfield and Jürgen Klopp was determined to quash it. Come the end of the 2019/20 season, 30 years would have passed since Liverpool had last been able to boast they were the best team in England. It had been a noose around the club's neck for way too long and it was tightening with every passing year. Seven managers had tried and failed to set them free.

As a European champion, Klopp's place in history was already assured, but bringing home the Premier League title would mean even more to a generation of Liverpudlians who had endured three decades of domestic mediocrity, laced with several near misses.

Having been so close the previous season, he was now firmly focused on breaking the Manchester City monopoly. Not even a club record 97-point haul in 2018/19 had been enough to overhaul it. Klopp knew it would require a season of near perfection to end their two-year stranglehold.

When the new league season kicked off, Liverpool burst out of the starting blocks to chalk up eight straight wins and establish themselves as the early pacesetters. Given the high standards City had set, the room for error was minimal and that bred a steely determination within the squad to grind out results, even when not at their best. By the time they travelled to Villa Park on the first weekend in November, they were still yet to be beaten and had opened up a six-point lead at the top.

Against a Villa side languishing in the lower half of the table, another three points were expected but the hosts took the lead midway through the first half and were still ahead as the game entered the closing stages.

For a team with serious hopes of winning the league, Klopp knew it wasn't good enough. "We had our good moments during the game but were not clinical enough, especially in the first half." The good work of the opening months was in danger of being undone.

"On days like this you just need to be ready to fight. After the first half we realised we were in the wrong path and we made changes," said the boss. With just three minutes left of the scheduled 90, though, it was still looking desperate until left-back Andy Robertson suddenly popped up at the far post to head the visitors level. It was only the third goal he'd ever scored for the club, and its importance cannot be overstated.

"I don't always believe we can win every game, but I never give up," said Klopp. Neither do his players. Four minutes into injury time, against all odds, Sadio Mané snatched a winner to complete another incredible comeback. The manager was obviously delighted but refused to get carried away. "We know we can do better," he acknowledged.

An ominous warning had been issued, however. Winning ugly can often be interpreted as a sign of potential champions and a significant psychological blow had been struck.

"We were a goal behind at half-time and went into the changing room wondering what the gaffer was going to say. Although he'd always get animated on the touchline, it was very rare for him to go overboard during the break and this was no exception. He remained calm and kept it brief, just a few simple instructions, but then made a loaded point about the white away shirts we were wearing and how they still looked so clean. Without him saying it outright, we all knew he wasn't happy with our performance. We took it on board, rolled our sleeves up and managed to turn things around. It's this subtle style of management that got the best out of us and he did it on so many occasions. For what he's done at this club, and all he achieved, he will go down as one of the all-time managerial greats."

ANDY ROBERTSON

HAND IT OVER

Liverpool v Manchester City | Premier League, 10 November 2019

Under Pep Guardiola, Manchester City were threatening to become the dominant force in the English game. They had claimed back-to-back titles and Klopp was not expecting them to relinquish their crown without a fight. This would be one of the most pivotal afternoons of the season.

The reigning champions arrived at Anfield six points adrift of league leaders Liverpool. A win for the hosts and that advantage would be stretched to nine, taking them a vital step closer to the object of their desire. Victory for the visitors and the gap would be back down to a worrying three.

The growing rivalry between the pair was intensifying and although City had pipped the Reds to the domestic title a season before, envious glances were cast

Below:
Bernardo Silva attempts to stop Andy Robertson as the top two go head-to-head at Anfield.

from the Etihad towards Anfield in June when the Champions League had been brought home. 'Klopp versus Pep', as it was billed in the media, was becoming the most hyped managerial duel in football and this latest episode didn't disappoint.

It began in spectacular fashion when, with only five minutes played, City had a penalty appeal turned down at the Kop end, from which Liverpool broke swiftly to open the scoring through an unstoppable 25-yard strike by Fabinho. Having drawn first blood, and with City temporarily on the ropes, Klopp's men ruthlessly doubled their lead minutes later through a Mo Salah header.

"If you want to win against City, you have to do something special and we had to be intense," explained the manager, and the high tempo he had set continued into the second half. Within just six minutes of the restart, Sadio Mané made it 3-0. Suddenly it felt like the Champions League quarter-final of 2018 all over again.

If he'd had any hair, Guardiola would have been tearing it out in frustration. His team did manage to grab a consolation goal, but the damage had been done. "What a game," said Klopp. "When City started to control it more in the last 15 minutes, it was tense, but then you saw the quality and what the boys can do. The boys did 75 minutes of unbelievable stuff."

The win not only extended Liverpool's lead over City, it also maintained a remarkable unbeaten run in the league that now stood at 29 games, their last defeat being at the Etihad the previous season. The home fans were buoyant. A sense of belief that this could finally be their season in the league rippled through the stands.

Yet the manager, while clearly delighted, was refusing to get carried away and did his best to play down the significance of these latest three points. "Who wants to be first in early November? It's important to be top in May," he stressed.

There were still two thirds of the season to play, and an intense period of fixtures loomed. However, given the lead they had, the title was fast becoming Liverpool's to lose.

Above left:
A warm embrace from the boss after Sadio Mané scores Liverpool's third.

Above right:
The goalscorer is mobbed by team-mates as the Reds extend their lead at the top.

Next page:
Manchester City boss Pep Guardiola shows his frustration on the Anfield touchline.

"Jürgen's team helped us to arrive at our limits. This is the truth. They have been our biggest rival, our biggest opponent by far. I've said many times I cannot define my period, our period here without them, impossible. I knew, from the moment he arrived at Liverpool, they would be real contenders and they became the biggest we had, miles away from the rest of the teams. I think, honestly, if I would be a football player, I would love to be his player. I admire him a lot, I have a lot of respect for him as a human being. This type of personality and charisma is unique, it's good for football. He changed Liverpool … he had to change players, had to change mentality, had to change moods. Liverpool gave him the time that every manager needs, and the results are there. Personally, he has been my best rival in football."

PEP GUARDIOLA

TOP OF THE WORLD

Liverpool v Flamengo | FIFA Club World Cup Final, 21 December 2019

The Club World Cup, in its various guises, has long divided opinion. A glamorous friendly at an unnecessary time of the season or a prestigious cup final that should be the pinnacle for all teams. In South America it's considered the holiest of grails. In Europe, not so much. Whichever way it's viewed, though, it remained a trophy Liverpool had never won.

In the early years, Liverpool didn't even bother entering. Then, when it was eventually deemed worthy of competing for, they returned home from tiresome trips to Tokyo in 1981 and 1984 wondering what all the fuss was about. By 2005, though, it was taken a lot more seriously and defeat in the final against São Paulo was a huge disappointment.

The 2019 competition in Qatar was a chance to right some past wrongs. Although he was far from happy with the scheduling – slap bang in the middle of the English league season – Klopp was looking forward to the challenge. "We

Above:
Roberto Firmino, the matchwinner, who sealed Liverpool's first-ever world title.

"In Brazil we really value the FIFA Club World Cup trophy a lot, unlike the English, who usually view the tournament as an inconvenience in the middle of a busy schedule. Ali, Fab and myself knew how seriously Flamengo would be taking this final so after a training session in Qatar we had a word with Jürgen to explain. Being the manager he is, one who always listened to his players, he took our comments fully on board and ensured the rest of the staff and team were aware of the importance too. It made a big difference and for me to then go on and score the winning goal that won the cup for Liverpool for the first time. This will always be one of my greatest memories in a red shirt. Obrigado Jürgen, you trusted me from day one and for this I will be eternally grateful."

ROBERTO FIRMINO

qualified, the boys wanted to play it, the club wanted to play it and I wanted to play it. That's why we are here, so now we should play."

It was Liverpool and Flamengo who won through to the final. Flamengo, the biggest club in Brazil, had denied Liverpool this title back in 1981 so there was a historic score to settle, while for a trio of Reds – Firmino, Alisson and Fabinho – there was, of course, added significance playing a team from their homeland.

At the pre-match meeting on the day of the game, Klopp outlined the importance of victory for the club and, given the controversy back home that had surrounded them being here, attempted to create a siege mentality among his players. The tournament clashed with a scheduled League Cup quarter-final at Aston Villa and Klopp's decision to prioritise Liverpool's quest for world domination sparked criticism from the English football authorities.

"Flamengo got sent here from their continent with a clear order to win it and to come back as heroes. We got told, 'Stay at home and play the Carabao Cup.'

Above:
The boys from
Brazil, Roberto
Firmino and
Alisson Becker,
with the FIFA
Club World Cup.

That's a massive difference. We cannot change that. Yes, we feel the tension in the situation. But we are here and we want to win the competition," he said.

Opportunities to become the best team on the planet don't come around very often so it was no surprise that a tense match ensued. Fittingly the winning goal came via the boot of Firmino, whose skill and composure broke the deadlock in the 9th minute of extra time to clinch a historic triumph.

The European champions were now World champions too and Klopp couldn't contain his pride or delight. "This is a wonderful night for the club and everybody who is with us. It feels outstanding, absolutely sensational. I am so proud of the boys. They keep getting tested and, at the moment, we're passing test after test after test."

Bill Shankly's long-held ambition to see Liverpool one day "conquer the bloody world" had finally been fulfilled and Jürgen Klopp's team were more than deserving of their place in the history books.

RUNAWAY LEADERS

Leicester City v Liverpool | Premier League, 26 December 2019

According to the so-called experts, this was to be the night when the Jürgen Klopp juggernaut finally hit the buffers. It was fast approaching 12 months since Liverpool had lost a league fixture and the nation was eagerly waiting to see them stopped in their tracks.

Just over 24 hours after returning from Qatar as the newly crowned world club champions, the long-time Premier League leaders were due to resume their title charge at Leicester with what should have been one of the season's most difficult fixtures.

After a 3,000-mile flight and the exertions of a month that had already seen them play seven times, the players were understandably shattered. Liverpool's chances of extending that lead at the top, against a side who were now their closest rivals in the table (albeit ten points behind), were being written off.

Below: Joe Gomez and Leicester's Jamie Vardy during the Boxing Day mauling of the Foxes.

Recognising that his team had been running on adrenaline and were in desperate need of a rest, Klopp made an inspired call to break with tradition, allowing the players to spend Christmas night at home with their families instead of staying over at a hotel the night before the game.

"He always seemed to be aware of any potential hurdles or pitfalls on the road ahead and coming off the back of such a big result out in Qatar, he really showed his appreciation for what we had just achieved in becoming world champions. Leicester away could have been difficult but he realised how much we needed a break and therefore altered the normal travel plans so we could spend Christmas at home with our families. Little gestures like that meant so much. He trusted us and treated us like adults, and that's why all the lads always wanted to give their all for him. He was such a great leader in this way. On a personal level, he's been way more than a manager to me. I've learnt so much from him. Apart from my close family, I can't think of a more influential figure in my life."

JOE GOMEZ

It was the best present the manager could have given them, and the difference it made was telling. Liverpool, contrary to what everyone was expecting, appeared refreshed, energised and hungry for three more points. The team repaid him with one of the best away performances in his time as manager, dominating proceedings from the first whistle. Roberto Firmino's goal gave them a 1-0 half-time lead but that was scant reward for how well they had played.

The second period continued in much the same vein, only this time Liverpool got their just reward. Three goals in seven scintillating minutes – from James Milner, Firmino again and Trent Alexander-Arnold – midway through the half made sure the scoreline reflected their dominance.

"That was exactly the performance we needed," said Klopp. "A little bit less good and we could have had problems. The boys were 100 per cent in the game and that helped a lot. We were very concentrated, and the goals were absolutely nice. An important day for us."

No team with a lead this big on Boxing Day had lost the Premier League before. Leicester boss Brendan Rodgers conceded that his former club would now "take some shifting". Liverpool were not yet at the halfway point of their league season and yet there was genuine talk of the red and white ribbons being prepared for their coronation.

Ever the professional, Klopp remained adamant that no-one at the club had mentioned or was even thinking about winning the title yet. "The only thing that changes are the numbers and now it is 13 points. We don't feel it. We just try with everything we have to be ready. The numbers are not relevant."

Still, it had been a highly profitable red Christmas for Jürgen Klopp and if his team could maintain pole position, then the greatest gift was still to come.

Opposite:
Jordan Henderson tries his luck during the impressive 4-0 win.

Above left:
A congratulatory arm around the shoulder from the boss for two-goal Roberto Firmino.

Above right:
Trent Alexander-Arnold celebrates with Jordan Henderson and Andy Robertson after scoring Liverpool's fourth.

KLOPP'S KIDS (1)

Liverpool v Everton | FA Cup 3rd round, 5 January 2020

Above: An
inexperienced
Liverpool
prepare to face
their local rivals
in the FA Cup.

Jürgen Klopp had never been afraid to give youth a chance but the starting eleven he selected for this FA Cup third-round tie at home to Everton was the cause of understandable concern among the fanbase.

Rotating his side for games at this early stage of cup competitions was nothing new. Just months into his Anfield tenure, Klopp had fielded what was then the club's youngest ever starting line-up against Plymouth Argyle. This was the Merseyside derby though, and there was more than a place in the next round at stake.

The Blues had not recorded a single win at Anfield since 1999 and Liverpudlians wanted it to remain that way. Eyes were fixed on the Premier League, but local bragging rights remained important too.

The manager, however, refused to be swayed by the emotion of parochial fervour. Klopp decided he had little option but to ring the changes.

It was a risk that could potentially have backfired, but he also had confidence in the depth of his squad. "If you want to be a Liverpool player, you have to respect the principles of this club," he said. "We cannot always play the best football in the world, but we can fight like nobody else."

The team he chose showed nine changes to that which had played the previous league game, with only James Milner and Joe Gomez retaining their place. It included two debutants, with a third coming on after just ten minutes, and four other players with a combined total of just nine previous starts between them. It was by no means the youngest team in Liverpool's history, but it was certainly the most inexperienced ever fielded for a Merseyside derby.

In contrast, Blues boss Carlo Ancelotti opted to play his strongest available eleven, but it never showed. "I saw a sensationally good performance of a not very experienced team with a lot of players playing for the first time on this kind of stage. It was outstanding," explained Klopp.

Above left:
A delighted Jürgen and young centre-back Nat Phillips following the 1-0 win.

Above right:
Neco Williams shows his ability to race past Everton's Lucas Digne.

Even after losing Milner, their most experienced player, with an early injury, this rookie Liverpool side never once wavered amid the heat of an intense battle. In the 71st minute, midfield starlet Curtis Jones stepped up to produce a moment of brilliance that was good enough to win the game.

Jones, a local lad and product of the club's Academy, wasn't even born the last time Everton had won at Anfield. Unfazed by the occasion, he stepped up to curl a sublime right-footed effort into the top corner and become the youngest goalscorer in a Merseyside derby since Robbie Fowler in 1994.

"All the kids played so well, I couldn't be more proud. I loved every second of it. A sensational game and a sensational goal from a Scouser – who could ask for more," beamed the boss afterwards.

His selection process had been fully justified and the legendary quip about the two best teams in this city being Liverpool and Liverpool reserves had never rung truer.

"As a local lad, playing in the derby was what I had dreamt about since being a kid, but if it hadn't been for the gaffer, I might never have played in it. I'd been ill beforehand, but he was always big on never showing weakness, so I kept it to myself and I'm so glad I did. This was massive for me and his advice to all the young lads that night was, 'Be cheeky, get on the ball, play the game and not the occasion.' With that in mind, I went out there and made the most of the opportunity. He was a big influence in bridging that gap between the Academy and the first team, and I've always looked up to him as a father figure. Whenever I had problems, on or off the pitch, he was always there to help. For me, he's been the perfect manager."

CURTIS JONES

AND NOW YOU'RE GONNA BELIEVE US

Liverpool v Manchester United | Premier League, 19 January 2020

It was the moment of sweeping realisation. A day when the pent-up emotions of the past 30 years were released in one almighty roar. Despite having been way out in front for most of the season, and the odds-on favourites to succeed Manchester City as champions, no-one at Liverpool, not least manager Jürgen Klopp, had been prepared to tempt fate by even contemplating it, until now.

Of the remaining fixtures, this was viewed as arguably the one with the most potential to throw a spanner in the works of the Reds' title-winning procession. It was at Old Trafford earlier in the season that Liverpool had dropped their only points and historic enmity dictated that United would be hellbent on trying to derail their fierce foes again.

Klopp and his players knew what a win here would mean. Virgil van Dijk's header gave them a first-half lead, but it wasn't until the very end that nerves were put at ease. Alisson Becker's long clearance sent Mo Salah racing clean through on the Kop goal and the league's most prolific marksman did what he does best to seal the points, sparking delirium in the stands, on the pitch and on the touchline.

"It's a big relief," admitted Klopp. "The boys were brilliant, taking responsibility for the dreams of so many people. We dominated the game, especially in the first half. The energy they put on the pitch was incredible. Then we scored a wonderful, wonderful goal at the end, so a really good feeling."

Within seconds of Salah's goal hitting the back of the net, it began, rising steadily and quickly turning into a crescendo that boomed out from every side of ground… "And Now You're Gonna Believe Us, We're Gonna Win The League." The message was loud and clear.

Opposite:
Virgil van Dijk jumps highest to head Liverpool into the lead against Manchester United.

Above:
Mo Salah's goal seals victory and takes the Reds 16 points clear at the top.

"They can sing that," said the manager, trying his best to keep a lid on his emotions. "I am not here to dictate what they sing. If our fans were not in a good mood now, that would be really strange. Of course, they are allowed to dream. But we will not be part of that party yet."

It was now a case of 'when' and not 'if', although Klopp was typically refusing to embrace such talk. "We are here to work. It is as simple as that. It is a very positive atmosphere, but I have to stay concentrated. Everybody can celebrate apart from us."

After all the hope, all the angst and all the doubt, the last big hurdle had been cleared and the finishing line was in sight. Victory over Manchester United had sent them 16 points clear at the top of the Premier League table, with the luxury of a game in hand.

For the fans at least, the shackles of superstition had finally been shed. Jürgen Klopp's team had entered the final straight and only a complete collapse could now stop them.

"Jürgen Klopp was seemingly born to be a Liverpool manager and had an instant connection with the club that very few can claim. Rather than buy a team of superstars, Klopp built a team of superstars. He re-established Liverpool as one of the biggest and best clubs in Europe but, as I knew only too well myself, it was the Premier League title that mattered so much. The pressure to end the long wait was massive, yet the squad he assembled was destined to do it. From very early in 2019/20 they looked like potential champions, and the victory over Manchester United at Anfield was the stand-out moment when belief finally and firmly replaced any doubt. This was one of the greatest Liverpool teams ever and they brought so much joy to a new generation. With the success Klopp achieved, not only did he make the people happy, he changed people's lives."

JAMIE CARRAGHER

BACK ON THE PERCH

Liverpool Crowned Premier League Champions, 25 June 2020

For one night only, blue was the colour and everyone of a red persuasion turned into a Chelsea supporter. Liverpool were potentially just a matter of hours away from being crowned champions of England for the first time in three decades and they could become so without kicking a ball. All eyes were on Stamford Bridge, where anything but a victory for Manchester City would send the title to Anfield.

Sensing this could finally be *the* night and one of the most significant moments in the club's history, Jürgen Klopp arranged for his entire playing squad and coaching staff to meet at the Formby Hall Golf Resort on the outskirts of the city. There, they would enjoy a barbecue and some drinks, watch the match on television and hopefully then be able to celebrate together.

"We did what we thought was right," recalled Klopp. "This will be forever and if something happens we have to be together otherwise we call each other and say 'oh congratulations'... That's not possible."

The world had, of course, changed immeasurably in the previous few months, with the Coronavirus pandemic bringing everything to a temporary standstill, including football. When the country was put into lockdown at the end of March 2020, Liverpool required just three more points to clinch the crown they had coveted for so long.

During a period of much uncertainty there was, for a spell, even talk of the season being cancelled. It was a worrying time. Thankfully, once restrictions began to ease slightly and the process of life returning to some sort of normality began, the Premier League eventually resumed in mid-June.

"When we went into lockdown, I didn't think about it for a second at all because it was not important at that moment," said Klopp, "but I became worried when people started talking about null and void. It was like 'wow!' I really felt it physically. That would have been really, really, really hard. You don't expect to get it as a present. We didn't want to have it on a points-per-game basis, so we were really happy when it was decided that we can play again."

With games being played behind closed doors, it was admittedly a strange experience but there was a title to be wrapped up and Liverpool didn't want to hang about. The first game back was a goalless draw away to Everton. The night before Chelsea hosted Manchester City, Klopp watched his side stylishly dismantle Crystal Palace 4-0 at Anfield.

After a brief pre-Covid wobble that resulted in a surprising first league loss of the campaign away to struggling Watford at the end of February, it was pleasing for Klopp to see Liverpool get back to winning ways. Even more impressive was the style in which victory had been achieved. It was a reminder of just how good they had been earlier in the season and a result that left Liverpool on the brink of their greatest achievement.

"That was important for the players, and I don't think it could have been better because my boys played like everybody was in the stadium," commented Klopp on the win over Palace. "The atmosphere on the pitch was incredible. That was the best counter-pressing game I have ever seen. The boys are in good shape and in a good mood. It was important we showed we are still here, and we do not want to wait. I was very happy; it gave me the 100 per cent feeling we will be fine."

While it would have been nice to clinch the title while actually playing, given everything that was happening outside of football and having waited this long, all that mattered now was getting the job done. So, on a sultry summer evening in late June, the manager and his players gathered on the outside patio area of the hotel, 13 miles from Anfield, and prepared to watch their destiny unfold before them.

Below:
Virgil van Dijk celebrates as Liverpool are confirmed as the 2019/20 Premier League champions.

Above: Jürgen and his squad proudly show off the flags that say Liverpool are champions.

"It started really relaxed," remembered the manager. "There was another game as well so we watched with one eye. We were eating barbecue then Chelsea and City started. Chelsea scored the first goal and there was celebration like I only usually saw when we score."

The cheers that greeted Christian Pulisic's 36th-minute goal in West London shattered the peace of this usually tranquil setting but Klopp was keen that his players didn't get too excited just yet, adding, "I didn't like that too much. It's too early, it's Man City and why do we celebrate like this?"

When Kevin de Bruyne equalised 10 minutes into the second half, momentum began to swing in City's favour and the champagne was put back on ice. As the game wore on, the tension rose, and so did the decibel levels on Merseyside whenever the home side attacked.

Then there was controversy over whether a Chelsea effort had crossed the line. The referee ruled it hadn't, but it appeared the ball had been handled in the area and VAR intervened. It all become too much for Alisson Becker, who, deciding his nerves couldn't take any more, got up and left.

After a two-minute delay, the ref pointed to the spot and Liverpudlians everywhere held their breath. Willian stepped up to take it. He stuttered slightly in the run-up then made no mistake with a rising shot that sent the keeper the wrong way. "The penalty goes in… celebration… and then just counting the minutes. It was just incredible," recalled Klopp.

Twelve minutes remained but there was no way back for City. "I called my family ten seconds before the end of the game and said, 'Okay, I love you all, I put the phone now on the table, leave your phone on and you can see what happens here.'

When the final whistle blew at Stamford Bridge, Formby Hall erupted. Across the city, car horns beeped non-stop, while fireworks lit up the night sky at a rapid rate. It was like the clock had just struck midnight on New Year's Eve but with much more meaning for Liverpudlians. What had long been deemed inevitable was now official.

With a record-breaking seven-game cushion, Liverpool Football Club were the 2019/20 Premier League champions, and Klopp was totally overcome with emotion. "Absolutely one of the best football moments I ever had in my life. It was absolutely exceptional," he said.

"You have no idea how it would feel before it happens. It was pure joy, massive relief in the next second and then I started crying. Then I wanted to speak to [my wife] Ulla and couldn't, I had her on the phone and I couldn't speak, I just was crying. I didn't know why it happened, I had no idea why, I couldn't stop. I never had a situation in my life when I couldn't stop crying and didn't know exactly why."

When his tears eventually dried, Klopp took a moment to reflect and let the magnitude of such a momentous occasion sink in. He had succeeded where his seven immediate predecessors had failed and ended the club's long and often laborious 30-year wait for a League title, one that some supporters feared they would never see again. His name would now forever be spoken in the same revered tones as the club's greatest-ever managers and, to top it all, his team had done it in sensational style to create a new history of their own.

"It's quite an achievement, but I feel overall relief," he said. "The big three-month gap, I did not know how we'd come back. There's no easy games in the Premier League … this is a big moment. I have no real words, to be honest. I am completely overwhelmed. I never thought it would feel like this. I had no idea. I could not be more proud of my players and coaching staff. Ever since we arrived it's been an amazing ride. And the fans, this is for you. We've done it together and it has been a joy. It's more than I ever dreamed of."

With his media duties out of the way, a well-deserved night of wild intoxicated celebrations followed. Klopp and his players, all sporting red home shirts with 'Champions 19/20' on the back, sang and danced long into the night. The Liver Bird was back on its perch and there was just one more thing left for Jürgen Klopp to do.

It was by now the early hours of the following morning, but he had one last phone call to make. It was to the person who can claim responsibility for ending Liverpool's domestic dominance back in the 1990s. "Hello … is that Sir Alex?"

Having missed a call from him earlier in the night, Klopp decided it was a good idea to give the former Manchester United boss a 3:30am wake-up call and gently remind him, in case he'd missed it, of the identity of the new Premier League champions.

"I think Liverpool were very lucky that Klopp came along when he did. A 'once in a lifetime' manager, that's what he is. The foundation of Liverpool came from Shankly's enthusiasm, and I think Klopp has got a lot of that, as well as personality and presence. He brought great unity to the club, entertainment into his teams and a determination not to give in. The demand to win a title must have been so great by the time they won it for the first time in 30 years. I felt that same pressure at United. We are friends so I tried to get hold of him and left a message, then he phoned me at three in the morning! He'd had a good night and said thanks for your message. I thought he probably doesn't know the time! Unbelievable. But I forgive him, at least he returned the call!"

SIR ALEX FERGUSON

"If someone had said back in 1990 that Liverpool wouldn't be champions again for 30 years, they'd have been laughed at. It needed someone special to end the drought and Jürgen was that man. An adopted Scouser who the supporters could instantly relate to, from the moment he came into the club, his positivity epitomised everything Liverpool stands for. This night was the culmination of what he had been working towards since becoming manager and no-one could begrudge him or his team this moment of recognition. To be stood on an empty Kop that night felt surreal but being asked to present the Premier League trophy was an honour and privilege. I remember Jürgen being more excited than anyone and he deserved to be. I said when he was appointed, 'fasten your seatbelts and get ready for take-off', and I wasn't wrong. He took us on some journey. Danke, Jürgen."

SIR KENNY DALGLISH

CORONATION

Liverpool v Chelsea | Premier League, 22 July 2020

This was the crowning moment of a season like no other. On the pitch it had been a glorious and unforgettable campaign. What happened off the pitch was unprecedented and, in the end, added to the drama. After 30 long years Liverpool had reclaimed their once proud mantle as the undisputed Kings of English football and they were about to reap the ultimate reward for their endeavours.

It was now late July, the time of year when players were normally back in pre-season training, but the new champions had one final home game to play, and they knew it would have a silver lining. "It's a little bit like Christmas," explained Jürgen Klopp beforehand. "It is a very important day and, yes, we are very excited."

The actual match was nothing more than a sideshow to the main event. The Reds raced into a three-goal lead before half-time before a late Chelsea rally threatened to spoil the party but, having worked so hard to get here, Klopp and his players were never going to allow that to happen. It eventually finished 5-3.

At any other time, the quality of the game would be discussed at length, but it was what came next that mattered most.

Below: Sir Kenny Dalglish congratulates Jürgen ahead of the Premier League trophy presentation.

Above:
Jürgen and the backroom team celebrate the Premier League success together.

Opposite:
A proud moment for the boss as he watches his captain lift the trophy.

Next page:
The thirty-year wait is over and Liverpool are champions of England once again.

It was the occasion every Kopite had dreamt of ever since Alan Hansen was presented with the First Division Championship at Anfield back in May 1990. At no point during the course of those three title-free decades, though, could anyone ever have imagined that the great red title drought would end like this.

An empty stadium in the middle of summer, a purpose-built stage on the Kop and compulsory face masks for those presenting the medals. Yet to finally see that much longed-for Premier League trophy at Anfield, with red and white ribbons tied to the handles and Liverpool's name engraved on the base, was both a sight for sore eyes and a welcome relief.

Fittingly, it was club legend Kenny Dalglish, the last manager to lead Liverpool to the title, who had been chosen to make the presentation. While it was a crying shame that no supporters were inside the stadium to share in this most precious of moments, when Jordan Henderson finally held the coveted prize aloft, it was only tears of joy that poured out as all the troubles of the past were washed away in a tidal wave of emotion.

"We really did it for them [the supporters]," said Klopp. "We celebrate here alone but we know everyone is celebrating with us at home. It's a great moment, an absolutely great moment. Becoming champions with this club is absolutely incredible. Being the manager is a big honour. I see it as pure luck. But it was some responsibility [to deliver the Premier League title] and obviously that fell off my shoulders in this moment."

Anfield glowed gloriously in the dark as the celebrations continued. It had been a memorable climax to a season that, for so many reasons, will never be forgotten.

THE BOSS MAN (1)

Jürgen Klopp named Manager of the Year 2019/20

There is no greater advocate of football being a team game than Jürgen Klopp; individual accolades don't rest easy on his shoulders. But after leading Liverpool to an incredible triple trophy haul in 2019/20, another honour quickly came his way and there could have been no more deserving recipient.

Twenty-four hours after his side brought the curtain down on a truly epic campaign by registering a record-equalling 32nd league victory of the season at Newcastle, it came as no surprise that Klopp was named Manager of the Year by the League Managers Association.

Following the season he had enjoyed, it couldn't have been given to anyone else. Even followers of Liverpool's bitterest rivals would not have begrudged him the award. It was a trophy to sit proudly alongside the UEFA Super Cup, FIFA Club World Cup and Premier League title, and he gratefully accepted it.

"I'm absolutely delighted to be named the winner of the League Managers Association manager of the year award, for this wonderful Sir Alex Ferguson trophy, named after a man that I admire so much," said the Liverpool boss.

The win at St James' Park meant Klopp's side had also set a new club record by finishing on 99 points, a huge 18 points clear of runners-up Manchester City. The amazing job he had done in the five seasons since taking charge at Liverpool was fully appreciated by everyone at Anfield, where the esteem in which he was held had now reached the levels previously only afforded to some of the illustrious names he had now emulated.

"It's an honour to be in the company of so many managers who have been named as LMA manager of the year before, including of course Liverpool managers like Bill Shankly, Bob Paisley, Joe Fagan, Sir Kenny Dalglish and, in recent years, Brendan Rodgers," added Klopp.

Typically, he was keen to divert the plaudits away from himself by drawing attention to the unsung contribution of all those who had helped him achieve the success that came Liverpool's way. "I am here on behalf of my coaches. I said it a lot of times, that I'm okay as a manager, but they make me, they make us, a really special bunch of football brains and I love to work with them. It's a pleasure.

Next page:
The 2019/20 Manager of the Year poses with his award at the club's Melwood training ground.

"We have so many great people here who made it happen that this year we won the title, and I only got this trophy because of that, I know. My players, all the people that I work together with, I take this and I love it for all of us together. Thank you very much. A very special season with a very special award in the end. Thank you, I am really honoured to get it."

"I will never forget the moment Jürgen called and asked me to return to the club. 'Together, we are going to conquer the world,' he told me. I didn't think he meant that literally but, of course, in 2019/20, we did. Not only that, we then went on to deliver the trophy everyone was desperate for. There was no limit to our success that season and it ended with Jürgen deservedly becoming manager of the year. Only a few coaches in the last 20 years have developed a style of football that defines an era like he did. To me he is a brother, a friend, a mentor, and together we have lots of good memories. He always said it's not what people think when you come in, it's what they think when you go out and Jürgen completely changed the identity of this club. He is the modern Shankly."

PEPIJN LIJNDERS

MENTALITY MONSTERS

2020–22

SEEING RED V THE BLUES

Everton v Liverpool | Premier League, 17 October 2020

For the first time in 30 years, Liverpool kicked off the 2020/21 league season as defending champions, Jürgen Klopp's players were in the unfamiliar position of being the team that everyone was desperate to prove themselves against.

The Reds had quickly got back into the winning groove; Mo Salah's hat-trick in a thrilling 4-3 win at home to newly promoted Leeds United on the opening day of the campaign was a particular highlight in what would become three straight league victories. Three notable new faces had strengthened the squad: Spain midfielder Thiago Alcantara from Bayern Munich and Portugal forward Diogo Jota from Wolverhampton Wanderers, as well as Greek full-back Kostas Tsimikas, who had been welcomed earlier in the summer.

At first glance, the team were issuing a warning to their rivals that wrestling the crown from their grasp was not going to be easy. But Covid restrictions meant games were still being played behind closed doors. Football just didn't feel the same, and before long the impact of this was being felt by Klopp and his team.

When Liverpool made the short trip to Goodison Park in mid-October, they did so off the back of a shuddering 7-2 defeat at Aston Villa. It was the worst loss the club had suffered in 57 years, and it raised more than a few eyebrows.

The team were ready to prove themselves against Everton, pressing hard to respond to that emphatic mauling in exactly the way Klopp wanted. They twice took the lead, through Sadio Mané after just three minutes and Mo Salah midway through the second half, only to be pegged back on each occasion.

"Performance-wise very, very happy. Best away game we've played here since I started managing," Klopp said.

But two controversial VAR decisions prevented the Reds from obtaining the victory they deserved. Klopp was irked by Jordan Henderson being denied a stoppage-time winner, and even more so by the serious knee injury sustained by Virgil van Dijk in the first half, which would have far-reaching consequences for the remainder of the season. Klopp believed Everton goalkeeper Jordan Pickford should have been shown a red card for a reckless lunge, but VAR only reviewed the incident for an offside. "We lost one player in a situation where VAR was not involved, with Virgil, and maybe another one in the red-card situation and scored a legitimate goal, which didn't count," seethed the boss afterwards. "The picture I saw was not offside, but it was because somebody decided it."

While having two points snatched from their grasp at the end was frustrating, it was the loss of his defensive lynchpin that upset Klopp most. The defender damaged ligaments in his knee and required surgery, ruling him out for the remainder of the season.

Van Dijk wouldn't be short of company in the treatment room. His injury began a domino effect; Liverpool players were soon dropping like flies as Klopp faced up to the biggest injury crisis of his managerial career.

"When you talk about Jürgen's qualities as a manager and where he ranks, he's certainly on the top table alongside the other great managers we've had at Anfield. He re-established Liverpool as one of the game's elite teams and took them back to the very top, at home and abroad. I remember in his first season, he had a clear plan of how to move the club forward and, after listening to what he said, I genuinely came away thinking, 'Wow, this manager and this person is an absolute superstar!' When you look at the transition from what Liverpool was then to what they became during his time in charge and how he leaves them, it has been nothing short of exceptional. He won stuff and he lost stuff but, more importantly, it's been a journey of enjoyment and that'll be his greatest legacy."

ROBBIE FOWLER

CRASH AND BURN

Liverpool v Burnley | Premier League, 21 January 2021

Anfield, the mighty impenetrable fortress of English and European football, was a pale shadow of its former self in 2020/21 and it's no coincidence that Jürgen Klopp's once all-conquering team suffered as a consequence.

There were, of course, other contributory factors for why Liverpool struggled this season. The long list of debilitating injuries that had begun with Virgil van Dijk's knee injury would eventually see 23 players being sidelined at one stage or another.

The exertions of recent years had also no doubt started to take their toll. The team had been operating at full pelt on a such a consistent basis at the highest level for a prolonged period, and so it was not unreasonable to expect a hangover of sorts at some point.

But it didn't take a genius to decipher that lack of support inside the stadium played a big part too. As the old adage goes, football without fans is nothing and for large parts of this campaign that's certainly how it felt in Liverpudlian eyes.

Without the unique sights and sounds of the Anfield crowd, there was no spark for the manager or players to feed off. It could be argued it was the same for every team at every ground, but nowhere was it felt more than here, where the '12th Man' had so often pulled the team over the line in times of trouble.

In January 2021, it was approaching four years since Liverpool had last lost at home in the Premier League – an incredible run of 68 games. Klopp's team had even managed to preserve the proud record of being unbeaten at home even whilst playing behind closed doors for the past six months. But if there ever was a time they needed the backing of their fans, it was now.

The reigning champions, who had topped the table as recently as the turn of the year, were in the midst of a slump. Five games without a league win and three without a goal, their confidence was draining fast. Lowly Burnley were the next

Opposite: Ashley Barnes, the Burnley striker who ended Liverpool's long unbeaten league run at Anfield.

Above: Roberto Firmino tries in vain to breach the Burnley rearguard.

visitors to Anfield and nobody expected them to threaten the Reds' invincible form in L4, but an Ashley Barnes penalty seven minutes from time clinched a historic victory for the visitors, which compounded the manager's misery.

Not since April 2017 had Klopp presided over a league loss on home soil. "A massive punch in the face," was how he described it. "A tough one, not easy to explain."

Liverpool were now clearly a team on the slide and dropped to fourth place. "If I sit now here, losing against Burnley, and talk about the title race, how silly would that be?" added Klopp.

It was to get worse. Over the course of the next two months, Liverpool inexplicably suffered a further five successive home defeats, erasing talk of the title for the season.

The boss wasn't one to look for excuses. If he had, then he'd have been spoilt for choice but an empty, soulless Anfield was certainly not helping matters. "Everything has been more difficult without fans," he lamented.

"Working for Jürgen was an invaluable learning opportunity for me from the first moment. Every conversation, every session, has been a masterclass. We all know how much the gaffer loves to counter-press and he put so much passion into this, during matches and on the training pitch. Just watching him generates enthusiasm. Being willing to constantly attack and be able to fight back is unique. As a coach you just try to take it all in and use it to form your own ideas. That's how it always was with Jürgen. I'm so grateful for how he welcomed me into the club, allowing me to work with this level of players, at this level of training and competition. I'll only ever feel honour and pride at being part of his project here. It's been an adventure of a lifetime and to share in all the memorable moments has been absolutely amazing."

VITOR MATOS

DIVINE INTERVENTION

West Bromwich Albion v Liverpool | Premier League, 16 May 2021

Desperate times call for desperate measures and the situation Liverpool found themselves in towards the tail end of the 2020/21 season was the most challenging yet of Jürgen Klopp's time at the club.

The defending champions had endured a campaign to forget. The continued absence of supporters in stadiums made for an uninspiring spectacle and a debilitating injury crisis contributed to the worst run of results the club had experienced during the Klopp era.

Nine league defeats – unheard of for a team that had lost only a handful of times in the previous three seasons – had long ended any hopes of retaining the title, while interest in the cup competitions had also ended prematurely.

This alarming fall-off in form threatened to have damaging consequences, though. With three games to go, the Reds sat 5th in the table and ran the very real risk of missing out on Champions League qualification. To do so would be a dramatic fall from grace for a club that had been champions of Europe just two seasons before.

Ahead of this trip to The Hawthorns, Liverpool's results had improved but it was imperative they kept on winning to have any chance of a top-four finish. After going behind early, Mo Salah equalised, but as the final whistle approached, it was still 1-1, a result that could have dashed all hopes.

Then, with literally seconds remaining, in one last desperate attempt to snatch those much needed extra two points, Alisson Becker went up for a corner. It was floated in from the left by Trent Alexander-Arnold and the keeper miraculously jumped highest to head home a sensational last-gasp winner. It was an extraordinary moment that almost defied belief and one that kept Liverpool's season alive.

"That game is our season in a nutshell," admitted a relieved Klopp. "We had to work like crazy but kept playing football and in the end we needed Alisson to sort it. I've never seen anything like that. It was an unbelievable header. The technique was insane. My part in the goal was that I didn't shout, 'Stay back!' I just let him run."

Following the sad passing of Alisson's father earlier that year, it was an emotional moment and one the boss, having recently lost his mother, could relate to. "We are really close, and I know exactly what it means to him. It's outstanding, really touching," he added. "It's only football but it means the world to us."

It also meant that Liverpool's chances of being back in the Champions League the following season remained in their own hands. The unlikely matchwinner had created history by becoming the first ever goalkeeper to score a competitive goal for the club and its importance can never be overstated.

"I remember when I spoke with him for the first time on a FaceTime video call, he just answered and started to smile, I started to smile, and we could already see that we would have a connection. He made the team feel comfortable but at the same time would put the necessary pressure on us. When I scored at West Brom, it was such an important and emotional moment. It meant so much. I dedicated the goal to my late father, and it was a thank-you to the boss too. Like myself, he had also been through a tough time personally but still found the time to support me when I needed it most. You never forget things like this. He is a great man as well as a great manager, and to have achieved so much together has been such a pleasure."

ALISSON BECKER

MISSION ACCOMPLISHED

Liverpool v Crystal Palace | Premier League, 23 May 2021

The 2020/21 season had been one to forget for a variety of reasons. But, on the final weekend of the Premier League campaign, Liverpool at least had the opportunity to salvage something tangible from it.

For the defending champions it was a massive come-down from what they had become accustomed to under Jürgen Klopp, a situation that seemed light years away from their recent silver-lined finishes. It was a hard-hitting reality check, but one that could have been worse.

Just a few months earlier their season had been completely written off, yet Klopp, against all odds, had somehow managed to pick his team up off the floor and drag them back into contention for a Champions League qualification spot.

After Alisson's heroics at West Brom, Liverpool went to Burnley for their penultimate fixture of the campaign. Young defender Nat Phillips was the stand-out performer in a 3-0 win that moved them back into the top four for the first time since February.

Their return to form had been timed to perfection. It meant they now only had to beat Crystal Palace at home on the final day to complete the job. "The past weeks and months have been good. We have played well. The boys have worked

Below left:
The Crystal Palace keeper denies Roberto Firmino on the final day of the 2020/21 season.

Below right:
A small section of the 10,000 supporters that were allowed back into Anfield for this game.

hard. But all of that was to help us to arrive in this position today. We don't make this bigger than it needs to be – it is big, we know it. And big games need big performances," wrote the manager in his programme notes.

Liverpool received the perfect pre-match boost ahead of this crucial visit when it was announced that up to 10,000 fans would be welcomed back to the stadium. With the crowd behind them, albeit only a fifth of what they were once used to, Klopp's players made no mistake.

With Gini Wijnaldum captaining the side on his final appearance for the club, goals either side of half-time from Sadio Mané rescued a season that otherwise would have been one of the most uninspiring in the club's history. "Outstanding," said Klopp. "Credit to the boys – I can't believe how it worked out in the last few weeks. We wanted this feeling, this game, this atmosphere. Incredible."

For the first time since 2018 there were no trophies to show for their efforts this year but, under the circumstances, the boss was more than satisfied. "Five, six or eight weeks ago, it was out of reach, barely possible. Fighting through this and finishing here in third is the best lesson you could learn in life. From nowhere to the Champions League in five weeks is a massive achievement."

In spite of everything that conspired against them in 2020/21 Jürgen Klopp's Liverpool had prevailed. They succeeded in attaining the bare minimum of their pre-season targets and, with a huge sigh of relief, would now regroup, ready to go again.

Above: Sadio Mané's two goals helped clinch victory and that all-important top-four finish.

Next page: Nat Phillips, a defensive rock during the run that secured Liverpool's Champions League qualification.

"To play for Liverpool is a great achievement but, for me, to say I've played for Jürgen Klopp's Liverpool takes it up another level. He was the first manager to show belief in me and I became a better player for the experience of working under him. I had to prove myself to a lot of people, but we always had a good understanding and he really put his trust in me towards the end of the 2020/21 season. There was big pressure on the club to secure Champions League qualification, but Klopp ensured it never got to the players. We went on a decent run and come the final day it just needed one last push. We got the result, and everyone could finally breathe again. To be part of a team managed by someone of his stature was a pleasure and something I will always be proud of."

NATHANIEL PHILLIPS

HIGH FIVE

Manchester United v Liverpool | Premier League, 24 October 2021

A sense of normality returned to football during the 2021/22 season. Supporters were finally welcomed back into stadiums and Liverpool were once again at the forefront of the hunt for the game's major honours.

Jürgen Klopp's team had put their troubles firmly behind them and embarked on a 16-game unbeaten run since the beginning of the season. It was like the clock had suddenly been switched back a couple of years, albeit with a few new faces, with central defender Ibrahima Konate having joined the team from RB Leipzig.

What hadn't changed was the pleasure Liverpudlians took in witnessing the seismic power shift between Liverpool and old rivals Manchester United. It was the events at Old Trafford in October 2021 that first highlighted the growing gulf between the country's two biggest, and traditionally most successful, clubs. Just like a local derby, there is always more than points at stake in a United game. That old cliché of form counting for nothing usually rings true.

Below:
Andy Robertson celebrates Naby Keita's opening goal in the 5-0 rout at Old Trafford.

Not this time, though. Liverpool went into the game flying high and brimming with confidence. United, meanwhile, were stalling, showing no signs of being involved in the title race. Home fans approached the game apprehensively, and their fears were justified.

This was Liverpool at the peak of their game, and they mercilessly tore United apart in front of the Stretford End. The home side were startled by the relentless pressing, swift counterattacks and ruthless finishing of Klopp's side. It was 2-0 inside the opening 13 minutes, with Naby Keita and Diogo Jota starting the rout before Mo Salah took centre stage in an incredible spell either side of half-time. Salah netted three times to become the first opposition player to score a Premier League hat-trick at Old Trafford, and the first Liverpool player to do so in any competition since 1936.

By the 50th minute it was well and truly game over. In front of their own fans, United had been totally humiliated. At 5-0 the visitors eased off slightly, content that the points were secure and history had been made.

Old Trafford emptied. Come the final whistle, a smattering of boos from the few diehards who stayed to brave the massacre were drowned out by laughter and songs of celebration as Liverpool supporters revelled in their club's best-ever victory at a venue that had so often before been a graveyard for their dreams.

Below:
Mo Salah makes it 3-0 as Liverpool romp to a famous victory.

Not even the most successful Liverpool teams had succeeded in embarrassing their fiercest rivals to this extent away from home. It was an afternoon that will never be forgotten.

"What can I say? Did I expect that? No. The result is insane," Klopp told the television cameras in the immediate aftermath. "It is a really good day, a big one. This is a little chapter in the history of the club. People will talk about it in the future because it won't happen again in a long time, if ever."

While the manager was right about how special a day it had been, he was wrong about one thing. Something similar, if not better, would happen again, and pretty soon.

"He's a fantastic manager who really took care of me when I first arrived. I recall we had a meeting and he explained how the team works. It was then down to me to prove I could be an important player for him on the field, and with his help that's what I did. I scored a lot of goals in my second season. One of the highlights was definitely the 5-0 win at Old Trafford and the boss deserves credit for the way he had us set up for that. Straight from the off we were on our toes and looking for space. Everything came naturally, and the two early goals really helped. He wanted us to keep attacking and in the end we could have scored more than the five we did. For me, that first-half performance was one of the best we played under him."

DIOGO JOTA

EURO STARS

AC Milan v Liverpool | Champions League Group Phase, 7 December 2021

Although there have been more important games between these two European giants, Liverpool's visit to the San Siro in early December 2021 was not without significance. It provided Jürgen Klopp and his team with an opportunity to reaffirm their status as one of the continent's elite clubs.

Having tamely exited the Champions League at the quarter-final stage against Real Madrid the previous season, Klopp wanted Liverpool to make amends and leave an indelible mark on the competition once again.

His first task, though, was to steer them through the potential minefield of the group phase. On previous occasions it had sometimes gone down to the wire, other times progress was more straightforward. This season certainly fell into the latter category.

Below: Mo Salah scores to draw Liverpool level in the San Siro.

Drawn alongside two fellow former multiple European champions, Milan and Porto, plus a strong Atletico Madrid side that had been beaten finalists twice in the previous eight years and who had eliminated Liverpool in the round of 16 two seasons before, it was considered to be the archetypal 'group of death'.

"Everywhere he goes you feel like, 'yeah, of course, it's his club, of course it's the perfect fit, of course they will fall in love with each other'. To come from behind, to overachieve, to be the hunter, to be the underdog. This is where he is the best. He injected the whole club like he did in Germany. He made Liverpool his club, his team and even his fans. That's what he does. You will always play against his aura, you will always play against the energy that he transports to his teams. You will always face a team that is on it from the first second and will not stop until they are all in the shower. It's so difficult but so nice to play against him because it brings out the best in yourself. It was always a pleasure. Our respect for each other grew a lot."

THOMAS TUCHEL

Klopp admitted he laughed sarcastically when first hearing the draw, but countered that with a confidence that suggested it held no fears for his team. "It's the Champions League, so that's how it is, and you have to play the best teams in Europe. It just so happens some of them are in our group," he said.

Any concerns the supporters may have had were quickly dispelled as Liverpool made a mockery of the media assumption they may struggle. An opening win at home to Milan was followed by impressive victories on the road in Portugal and Spain, results that were then repeated in the corresponding fixtures at Anfield.

Five successive wins comfortably guaranteed qualification, while top spot in the group was also secured with ease. This meant there was nothing riding on the final game in Italy, but for Jürgen Klopp and his players, there remained a chance to make an emphatic statement. No English club had managed to win all six Champions League group games before, and the boss was determined for his team to seize the moment.

Although changes to the team were inevitable, the side he chose was stronger than expected. "We want to field the best possible side for the situation we are in, but we want to win the game," said the boss. With Milan still not assured of qualification, it wasn't going to be easy and it was the hosts who opened the scoring just before the half-hour mark. Mo Salah then drew Liverpool level and, early in the second half, Divock Origi made it 2-1.

Liverpool finished the group a massive 11 points clear of second-placed Atletico, completing their fixtures with a 100 per cent record and leaving the manager beaming with pride. "What the boys did, I could not be more proud. It was an incredible game, the performance was outstanding and I am so happy, especially because of the sixth game."

Another Jürgen Klopp-inspired European adventure was well underway and it had begun with more history being made.

SPOT ON

Liverpool v Chelsea | League Cup Final, 27 February 2022

As Jürgen Klopp would later explain, following Liverpool isn't all about the glory, it's about the journey. As the business end of the 2021/22 season approached, it was shaping up to be yet another exhilarating ride. His team had a four-way ticket to potential success and the first major stop on the route was a familiar one.

Wembley Stadium is a venue inextricably linked with some of this club's greatest moments. Such was the regularity with which Liverpudlians once travelled there, it was famously dubbed 'Anfield South'. In late February 2022, they headed back there in their thousands to see if Klopp could win at the iconic venue for the first time.

After a rare trophyless campaign the season before, the manager was eager for his team to get back in the habit of collecting silverware. "We all know that in the moment people are really happy with this team," he said. "But in 20 years, if we don't win anything else, people will say, 'Yeah they were good, but they should have won more.' That's why we should now try again to win a few things."

It was at the same place and in the same competition six years before that Klopp experienced the first notable disappointment of his Liverpool journey, but he and the team had come a long way since then. Reaching cup finals was no longer a novelty.

Waiting for them beneath the arch was Thomas Tuchel's Chelsea, a side they had drawn with twice in the league. In preparation for the final, the manager and his staff reviewed those two games and came away encouraged by what they saw, with the manager saying privately: "The most important message is that we can still improve."

As usual, a tactical plan was devised, which the coaches then relayed to the players. But when the boss spoke at the team meeting a day before the final, he opted to keep things brief and signed off by simply reminding them that he was talking to "the best football team in the world". On the day of the game, despite the scale of the occasion, he added, "Just do the things we always do."

It turned out to be an epic, incident-packed encounter. Both teams went at it right from the first whistle and the action was end-to-end throughout. Chances were missed, saves were made, posts were struck and goals were disallowed, with VAR ruling out a Joel Matip header and the referee chalking off three Chelsea efforts. The pace was frantic and intensity levels rarely dropped.

Unbelievably, after 90 minutes and extra time, it finished goalless. "It was like two lions absolutely going for each other. It was absolutely crazy and in the end

everyone on the pitch was obviously very tired," said Klopp. Given that the teams had put so much into the game, penalties seemed a harsh way to decide the destiny of the trophy and even that proved to be a lengthy process.

Fortunately, Liverpool had been preparing for an outcome like this ever since Klopp invited German neuroscience company neuro11 to start working with them at the club's summer training camp. This involved analysing brain activity during training drills to help a player's mindset for in-game set-piece situations such as penalties. The manager described it as a "very interesting new chapter for us" and its impact was about to be put to the ultimate test.

Milner, Fabinho, Van Dijk, Alexander-Arnold and Salah successfully converted Liverpool's first five penalty kicks, only for Chelsea to do exactly the same, meaning it went to sudden death. Jota, Origi, Robertson, Elliott and Konate then all scored too but again each of their efforts were subsequently cancelled out.

Up next stepped goalkeeper Caoimhin Kelleher. Klopp had stuck to his word that Kelleher, who had kept goal in all the previous rounds, would retain his place for the final. "Even in professional football there should be space for some sentiment," said the boss. "Kelleher is a young boy, plays in all the competition, what do I do? I am a professional manager and a human being and the human being won. He deserves it."

Klopp's faith was rewarded with a man-of-the-match performance from the young Irishman and the crowning moment was yet to come. "For me Alisson Becker is the best goalkeeper in the world and if I'm being honest Caoimhin Kelleher is the best number two in the world, especially for the way we play, and he had an incredible game."

A forward player in his youth, Kelleher showed that he had not lost his eye for goal when expertly blasting home the spot kick that left Liverpool on the brink of

Above left:
Joel Matip scores with a header but this effort is ruled out by VAR.

Above right:
James Milner prepares to take Liverpool's first penalty in the shoot-out.

"He's the only manager I've known here and obviously it was him who gave me my opportunity, along with a number of other lads from the Academy, so he's been brilliant, to be fair. He's helped bring us all on and filled us with the belief that has enabled us to grow. His advice to me has always been quite simple. He recognises that when it comes to preparing for a game, I'm one of those players who just likes to do my own thing, so even before the first League Cup Final in 2022, he gave me a simple idea of how he wanted me to play, then had the confidence to just let me get on with it in my own way and that all contributed to what was a massive moment in my career."

CAOIMHIN KELLEHER

victory yet again. Roles were now reversed, and it was Kelleher's turn to try and deny his opposite number Kepa Arrizabalaga, who had only been brought on as substitute in the final minute of extra time due to his reputation as a penalty-saving expert. That had obviously already backfired, and when he then blazed his kick high over the bar, the match was eventually settled, 11-10 in Liverpool's favour.

"The penalty shoot-out was one of the most spectacular I ever saw, and it was absolutely great to win it like this. What I love most about it is that the whole squad had been part of the journey," added Klopp.

Liverpool were Wembley winners once again and the subsequent celebrations showed just what it meant. It was the club's first domestic cup success in a decade and their ninth League Cup Final win overall, making them the most successful club in the competition's history. For Jürgen Klopp, his team were back on the trophy-winning trail, and it was another important step on that journey he would constantly refer to this season.

"The phrase 'glory hunter' can often be tagged to those drawn to following certain clubs," he said. "The point was with Liverpool it's different. It's not 'glory hunting', it's 'journey hunting'. It is about the journey and we are on it."

Above left:
Goalkeeper
Caoimhin
Kelleher scores
from the spot to
make it 11-10.

Above right:
The Wembley
hero shows
off the cup to
supporters.

I'M SO GLAD

Liverpool v Manchester City | FA Cup semi-final, 16 April 2022

Although Jürgen Klopp was loath to talk about it, Liverpool's quest for an unprecedented quadruple was rapidly gaining momentum. If they could pass what was deemed to be the sternest test of their credentials yet, he knew it would intensify.

Having already won the League Cup, Liverpool were the only side in with a chance of becoming the first to scoop all the major trophies in one season. A place in the last four of the Champions League had recently been secured, while in the Premier League they were second, locked in a fascinating battle with their FA Cup semi-final opponents Manchester City. A week earlier they had drawn 2-2 in a thrilling encounter at the Etihad, and just one point separated them.

Now, the undisputed best two teams in the country were going head-to-head at Wembley for a place in English football's showpiece event. It was a game that would have graced the final itself and it more than lived up to the pre-match hype surrounding it.

City started as favourites but Klopp, while maintaining respect for the opposition, wasn't concerned. "We respect City so much and it's so difficult to win against them. But because we have these boys in our dressing room we have a chance," he said.

For almost everyone at the club, including himself, playing in the FA Cup semi-final would be a new experience and on the morning of the game Klopp told his players: "Make it special by being normal. We are historically very lively against them."

Below left:
Jürgen listens as the fans serenade him with their new song.

Below right:
Andy Robertson floats in the corner from which Ibrahima Konate scores the opening goal.

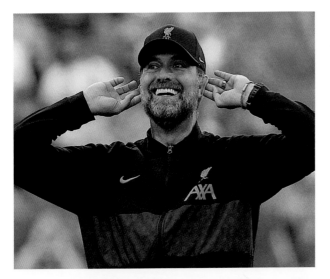

Given the way Liverpool started this game, 'lively' was an understatement. In the baking Wembley sun, City wilted under the intense pressure exerted by the Reds, who ruthlessly swept their opponents aside with a totally dominant first-half display.

Ibrahima Konate headed in the first goal after only nine minutes before man-of-the-match Sadio Mané netted twice to make it 3-0 at the interval. "The first half was one of the best we ever played," admitted Klopp. "We did all the right stuff, we scored in the right moments. We were outstanding. I loved each second of it."

On the Wembley concourse at half-time, jubilant Liverpudlians sang non-stop. To the tune of the Beatles classic 'I Feel Fine' they belted out what was fast becoming the new soundtrack to Liverpool's season.

The majority were still singing downstairs when City hit back with a goal immediately after the restart. They later reduced the deficit again in injury time. Nerves frayed, but it was too late and Liverpool deservedly hung on for a famous victory.

"Absolutely proud, incredible," said Klopp. "I think City knew beforehand that it could be difficult against us. That's how it has been between us most of the time. But we beat the strongest team in the world and that's a pretty special moment."

Klopp reiterated that he still didn't believe the quadruple was possible, but after this performance one thing was for certain: Liverpool supporters were even more glad Jürgen was a red.

Above: Man-of-the-match Sadio Mané celebrates after increasing Liverpool's lead with two first-half goals.

Next page: Centre-back Ibrahima Konate, whose 9th-minute goal set Liverpool up for a memorable victory.

"He's done a lot for me. First of all, by bringing me to this magical club and then by helping me become the player I am today. When I first arrived, I was only 22 and to sign for Liverpool at such a young age was a dream come true. Every day working with Jürgen Klopp then helped me become a better player, even if sometimes he had to kick my ass! One of the most memorable games in my first season was the semi-final of the FA Cup, at Wembley Stadium, and I scored a goal just after the start. It was from a set-piece that the boss and his coaching staff had been working with us on in training. For it to pay off in such an important game was incredible and he was very happy afterwards, especially as it set us up for a famous win."

IBRAHIMA KONATE

SINKING THE YELLOW SUB

Villarreal v Liverpool | Champions League semi-final 2nd leg, 3 May 2022

Jürgen Klopp's Liverpool rarely did things the easy way. What should have been a comfortable passage into their third Champions League Final in five years typified this. They travelled to Spain's east coast armed with a 2-0 first-leg lead yet somehow almost managed to throw it away.

Amid heightening talk of the quadruple and with a hectic run of games looming, the hard work for this game had seemingly already been done at Anfield, leaving this as one of the less intense fixtures that remained. But Villarreal had eliminated Juventus and Bayern Munich in earlier rounds, and this wouldn't be easy.

The boss instructed his players to treat this game as if the tie was still goalless. "Beforehand I told the boys I'd like to read the headline 'Mentality monsters were

in town', because I wanted us to be the ones who went for the result and not defend," he said.

At the compact and atmospheric El Madrigal though, Klopp's team were in for a rude awakening. During a dismal first-half display, Liverpool's hopes of reaching the final looked in danger of being washed away with the incessant rain that had been falling throughout the day. Inside three minutes the deficit had been halved and then by the interval wiped out altogether. Liverpool were grateful to reach half-time.

It required the inspired introduction of substitute Luis Diaz, some tactical tweaks and a few wise words from the manager to stop the rot. "The whole world now thinks it goes in one direction. We are the only team who can change this. Don't be frustrated. It's time to show that we will earn the right to be playing in the final," Klopp told the team.

The mentality monsters, a phrase first coined by the boss back in the 2018/19 season, were about to prove their mettle. The second half saw a much improved

Opposite: Liverpool number one Alisson Becker during the Champions League semi-final 2nd leg.

Above: Jürgen passes on some tactical advice to Virgil van Dijk against Villarreal.

Liverpool performance and when Fabinho restored their aggregate advantage shortly after the hour mark, there was no looking back.

Just a minute after hitting the woodwork, Diaz then scored with a back-post header to make it 2-2 and further ease any nerves, before the pace of Sadio Mané saw him race clean through on goal and roll the ball into an empty net to seal Liverpool's place in the Paris final.

"It is outstanding," said Klopp. "We made it pretty tricky for ourselves. We knew before that these kind of things can happen. In life it is always about how you react when things don't go your way. It is really difficult to reach three finals (in one season), which is probably the reason why no-one did it so far but we made it happen. It's massive."

In taking Liverpool through to a third Champions League Final Jürgen Klopp had emulated Anfield great Bob Paisley, and it would be his fourth final appearance in total, a feat only accomplished by Marcello Lippi, Sir Alex Ferguson and Carlo Ancelotti. Esteemed company, in which he no longer seemed out of place.

Below: The introduction of substitute Luis Diaz helped turn the tie back in Liverpool's favour.

"The moment I came off the bench against Villarreal in the Champions League for me was very special because we were two goals behind, and I proved that the manager was right to put his trust in me. He told me to go out onto that pitch and do what I know best. We were fighting to stay in the competition and reach the final, so it was really nice to come on and help the team turn the result around. I will always be grateful to him for allowing me to play my football with joy and happiness. As long as we also adhered to tactical plans and instructions, he was like that with every player and for me that is very important. From the day I arrived, until the day he left, to play for him at this great club has been an incredible experience."

LUIS DIAZ

WEMBLEY WIZARDS

Liverpool v Chelsea | FA Cup Final, 14 May 2022

Until 2022, Jürgen Klopp and the Football Association Challenge Cup had not enjoyed the best of relationships. From accusations he had disrespected the world's oldest and most prestigious knockout competition by allegedly fielding weakened teams in the past, to the fact his side had only once, in six seasons, progressed beyond the fourth-round stage, it had been a source of irritation and frustration.

While there could be no denying that Klopp's record in the FA Cup since joining Liverpool paled in comparison to what he had achieved in other competitions, it certainly wasn't for a lack of trying and the manager was well aware of what it would mean for his club to lift this trophy for the first time since 2006.

"People always said I'm not the biggest fan of the domestic cup competitions – that's not true, it just never happened," explained Klopp. "It started as a similar experience [to other competitions] but ended earlier."

With a squad that now boasted much greater strength in depth than ever before, the draws for the earlier rounds were kind and everything seemed to click as they advanced past Shrewsbury Town, Cardiff City, Norwich City and Nottingham Forest towards that famous semi-final victory over Manchester City. "This year is different," Klopp said. "It has been really special and it is a big one for us."

Their successful FA Cup run went hand-in-hand with the momentum that was carrying them through the challenges on other fronts. They travelled south for English football's showpiece event still in with a chance of sweeping the board. Waiting for them at Wembley were familiar foes Chelsea, determined to avenge their League Cup Final defeat earlier in the season and scupper Liverpool's quest for the quadruple.

Although it was the most hectic season he had known (this was their 60th game), Klopp admitted he wouldn't have it any other way. "It is pure joy to be part of this club at the moment," he said. "We came from a season last year where nobody, apart from me, thought we could go again like we did this year. There is a lot to come and a lot to play for."

On this occasion, with two massive Premier League games and a Champions League Final on the horizon, Klopp could have been forgiven for prioritising the upcoming challenges, but he remained adamant that they were all being treated with equal importance.

Above:
Liverpool
and Chelsea
line up at
Wembley
ahead of the
2022 FA
Cup Final.

"Until now, it's the first time ever a team fought for the title and was in three finals. The decisive part is coming now. It's really difficult and really intense but no problem at all. Being here is good, but the icing on the cake is still missing and we are working on that now."

The FA Cup was, of course, the one domestic trophy missing from his collection, and he added: "It is our first one [FA Cup Final] and we are a different kind of team than we were in the past. These boys are now really ready to go for the biggest prizes and the FA Cup is a massive prize. So, we will try to be the best version of ourselves and bring it home."

Like the League Cup Final, it was to be another tight and tense afternoon that could have gone either way. Both sides created opportunities to score and Liverpool, who lost Mo Salah and Virgil van Dijk through injury, twice hit the woodwork. After 120 minutes, there were, once again, no goals to show and a penalty shoot-out was required to decide the destiny of the trophy.

James Milner, Thiago Alcantara, Roberto Firmino and Trent Alexander-Arnold all held their nerve to score. With Chelsea having missed their second kick, Sadio Mané had the chance to win the cup for Liverpool, only for his shot to be saved. Klopp held his hands up and later admitted he was partly to blame, explaining: "Sadio's penalty was 50 per cent my responsibility. I said to him that the goalie [Édouard Mendy] knows you, so go the other way. Not for the first time in my life I realised I should have shut up."

In sudden death the balance swung in Chelsea's favour, but Diogo Jota then netted and Alisson Becker kept out Mason Mount's effort, meaning the

responsibility to clinch victory now fell on the shoulders of Kostas Tsimikas. The self-proclaimed 'Greek Scouser', who had come on as a substitute in extra time, showed no fear and sent the keeper the wrong way to spark yet more jubilant scenes beneath the Wembley arch.

A fog of red smoke filled the air and while Liverpudlians partied in the stands once more, Klopp danced and hugged his players and staff on the pitch. For the manager, it had been another special day.

"We saw before the game what it meant to people because our hotel is pretty central and they were partying from this morning," he said. "I couldn't be more proud of my boys, the shift they put in and how hard they fought. They were outstanding. It was an incredible, intense game and then in the penalty shoot-out, it was nerve-racking. My nails are gone but I really feel for Chelsea – for the second time, 120 minutes and you get nothing, that's how small the margins are and it's hard. But in the end there must be one winner and that was us, so I'm pretty happy. It's massive for us."

The FA Cup was returning to Anfield for an eighth time, the first since 2006, and Jürgen Klopp had completed his domestic set of trophy wins, the first manager in Liverpool's history to do so.

"Winning the FA Cup is the best memory I have in football. For me, it was something so special and I thank Jürgen Klopp for giving me that opportunity. He thought I was going to take one of the first penalties but when he asked me I said I want to take the seventh. I chose that because I had only come into the game a few minutes before, and he was fine with that. Also, the previous night I had thought about this scenario and where I would put my penalty. I was really confident, stuck to it and scored. Afterwards, we didn't talk much about the game, we just celebrated together. To play for the best coach in the world has been a privilege and he did so much for my career. To repay him with that penalty and that trophy at Wembley was an amazing feeling."

KOSTAS TSIMIKAS

PIPPED AT THE POST

Liverpool v Wolverhampton Wanderers | Premier League, 22 May 2022

As the old saying goes, 'It's the hope that kills you.' On the final afternoon of the 2021/22 Premier League season, everyone connected to Liverpool Football Club would painfully discover the true meaning of this.

Having lifted the FA Cup at Wembley, Jürgen Klopp's Liverpool had kept the title race alive with a midweek victory at Southampton and now faced a day of destiny at home to Wolves.

Liverpool were now just two games away from winning four trophies in a season, and questions around this most historic of achievements were becoming difficult to ignore.

Realistically though, the third leg of this potential quadruple remained a tall order. Manchester City were in pole position, with Liverpool a point behind. All they could do was beat Wolves and hope that an Aston Villa side managed by Kop legend Steven Gerrard could do them a favour at the Etihad.

The manager and his players had helped supporters believe that anything was possible and a carnival atmosphere greeted the double cup winners. An early goal by Wolves dampened the mood but Sadio Mané levelled. As half-time approached, news filtered through that Villa had taken the lead in Manchester. Midway through

the second half, ex-Red Philippe Coutinho doubled Villa's advantage and Anfield was whipped into a frenzy.

For a brief moment the dream flickered, only to be quickly extinguished when, in the space of 12 minutes, City completed a remarkable comeback that rendered late goals by Mo Salah and Andy Robertson meaningless.

So near, yet so far. It had been an emotionally draining afternoon. "I wasn't really aware of the full story," reflected Klopp. "There was one moment when it was 3-2 and I don't know why but we thought they [Villa] had equalised again. With all the things that happened, I would have preferred them [City] to be 5-0 up after 10 minutes, to be honest."

The quadruple was no more, but Klopp was quick to stress the positives. "The boys have played an incredible season. Ninety-two points is crazy. The whole journey, it's absolutely exceptional. The season was so tight. What I've learnt about life is if you stay on track and keep going, you get your rewards. Not today, but we will get it."

Liverpool had given it their best shot, only to be pipped at the post by Manchester City for the second time in four years, but the boss managed to remain magnanimous in defeat. "It was clear before the game a lot of things had to happen [for Liverpool to win the title]. Congratulations to Man City, Pep Guardiola, their players. We were close but in the end not close enough."

On the Kop a banner had been unfurled that simply read 'We Win Cups'. With two already in the bag and hopefully a third to come, it was a reminder, if needed, that despite this disappointment, it had still been a season to savour.

Above: The flags are out in force on the Kop for the last home game of 2021/22.

Next page: Luis Diaz attempts to win the ball from Jonny of Wolves.

"I've been fortunate in my career to come up against some outstanding managers and Jürgen is obviously one of those. You always knew that his team would give its all. They epitomised what the supporters want: to fight, to run but also to play quality football. Jürgen very much embraced that at Liverpool. The pressing was incredible. They were a very physical team, full of speed and full of aggression. This allowed the tempo of the game to always be very high and they could really hurt teams. Naturally, there were changes within the squad over time, but keeping that core of players together was key. When I look back at Jürgen's time, he gave absolutely everything, and more, to the club, and won absolutely everything. For me, he goes down as one of the real managerial greats at Liverpool and of the Premier League era."

BRENDAN RODGERS

HEARTACHE IN PARIS

Liverpool v Real Madrid | Champions League Final, 28 May 2022

The romantic notion was that Paris in spring would rekindle a long-lasting love affair and consummate the greatest season of Jürgen Klopp's time at the club.

It had been three years since Klopp had last set eyes on the trophy that first captured Liverpudlian hearts in 1977. If he could bring it back to Anfield for a seventh time, the heartache of being jilted at the Premier League altar would quickly be forgotten.

Below: Despite dominating for long periods, it was a frustrating night for the Reds in Paris.

Opposite: Jürgen consoles Naby Keita after Liverpool's Champions League Final loss to Real Madrid.

Any trip to the French capital at this time of year will always evoke heartwarming memories of Alan 'Barney Rubble' Kennedy's goal at the Parc des Princes and Phil Thompson hoisting European Cup number three into the Parisian sky. And, just like in 1981, Real Madrid would provide the opposition once again.

The 13-time champions of Europe could, of course, boast about their own special relationship with this trophy, one that dates back to the inception of the competition in the mid-1950s. Their last kiss had come at the expense of Liverpool in Kyiv in 2018.

Everything was set up for a classic encounter at the Stade de France, the third instalment of European Cup Final trilogy that began in this city four decades ago. Historically, the score was 1-1, with both clubs keen to settle old scores. "There's

"Our teams played a lot against each other and, of course, with Real Madrid, I have good memories of the final in 2022. To win the Champions League is the best that can happen to you in your career. Little details can decide if you win or not and, against Liverpool in this competition, I have a big history. To play against Jürgen's team in Paris was really complicated because of how they press. It's difficult to find a team that presses with such intensity, so the key for us was to avoid giving their front line space. We won that game but for his personality and style of football, Jürgen was the best manager Liverpool could have. To keep Liverpool at the top for nine years was fantastic, playing really well with an entertaining team. He's a funny guy, an honest guy who I respect a lot as a manager and a person."

CARLO ANCELOTTI

the feeling that we want to put things right, definitely, but it cannot be the main thought," warned Klopp.

In the build-up to kick-off, excitement and confidence were high but the mood suddenly soured when chaos at the turnstiles outside the Liverpool end of the stadium caused thousands of supporters to be locked out. It resulted in the start of the game being delayed by 36 minutes and clearly made for a more subdued atmosphere.

Despite having 23 shots on target compared to Real Madrid's three, Liverpool came up against a keeper in sensational form. Their best opportunity came when Sadio Mané's first-half shot was tipped onto the post. In what was Liverpool's 63rd game of the season, the spark that had carried them this far just couldn't be re-ignited, They were eventually punished just before the hour mark when the decisive moment of the night fell to Vinicius Junior. It proved to be the winner and a season of so much promise ended in double disappointment.

"They scored a goal, we didn't. That's the easiest explanation in the world of football and it's hard," was Klopp's honest post-match assessment. "In the last third we could have done better. I saw us doing really a lot of good things, but it was not enough, and we take that. I told the boys in the dressing room that all I feel is pride. They played an outstanding season. The two competitions we couldn't win, we were denied by the smallest possible margins."

On and off the pitch it had been a hugely frustrating night. The course of true love never runs smooth and Liverpool's experience of Paris in 2022 was most definitely one to forget.

Above: Carlo Ancelotti, the architect of Liverpool's 2022 Champions League final heartache.

RETURN OF THE RED HEROES

Liverpool's Homecoming Parade, 29 May 2022

Half a million people can't be wrong. Despite having missed out on a historic quadruple, Liverpool's 2021/22 season was deemed more than worthy of a celebration. When Jürgen Klopp and his team returned home to Liverpool less than 24 hours after suffering the disappointment of defeat, the people partied like it was 2019 all over again.

The pain of Paris remained raw, as did the memories of narrowly missing out on the Premier League title a week before, but this proved to be the perfect antidote, described at the time as 'like a big Scouse hug'.

Although Liverpool had the League Cup and FA Cup to show for their efforts, there had been more than a few reservations expressed about whether it was still right to proceed with the parade and how it would be received. Some players were genuinely concerned that it could be thrown back in their face, but they needn't have worried.

The scenes that greeted the double cup winners left Klopp visibly gobsmacked. "You have to plan these type of things and we hoped we would find something like this, something incredible. Yes, we lost the last two trophies, but these people don't forget. They know exactly what shift the boys put in." said the boss.

Helping to lift the mood further was world-renowned DJ and Liverpool supporter Calvin Harris who, from his position on the decks at the back of the bus, provided the perfect soundtrack to an uplifting and unforgettable four hours. Performing a set that included the club's unofficial anthem 'One Kiss', he had the bus rocking all the way.

Below left:
Liverpool-supporting DJ Calvin Harris entertains the team on their return from Paris.

Below right:
An amazing reception greeted the beaten Champions League finalists on their return home.

"One of the main characteristics of a Klopp team is the intensity at which they play, and his Liverpool were one of the best at this. I remember when I was Liverpool manager, we played against his Mainz side in a pre-season friendly and what struck me straight away was the intensity in their play. He continued this throughout his career and took it to another level at Anfield. When he became manager here I knew it was a fine appointment because you could tell someone with his character would connect with the fans and the people of this city. With the passion he has, it came as no surprise that they loved and respected him. He gradually built the team up to the point where they were competing and winning consistently again. To win any trophy as manager is unbelievable but to win the amount he did is amazing."

RAFAEL BENITEZ

The sights along the tour route were reminiscent of what Klopp and the players had experienced three years earlier when they returned home as European champions. An estimated 500,000 lined the streets and every vantage point was occupied, some more perilously than others. For as far as the eye could see, it seemed as though a massive red blanket had smothered the city once again.

"When you see the eyes of the people, it really is incredible," said the manager. "You don't have to win, you just have to put all that you have in and the people of Liverpool love you. I am proud of these players, but I am just as proud of these people too. Lose the Champions League Final the night before and the people arrive here in the mood they are. It is absolutely outstanding. This is the best club in the world. I don't care what people think. I'm not drunk, just emotional."

After a marathon 63 games that yielded a thrilling title charge, three cup finals and two trophies, it was finally time for everyone to take a deep breath. For Jürgen Klopp's journey-hunting mentality monsters, another remarkable season was over, and their sterling efforts had not gone unappreciated.

THE BOSS MAN (2)

Jürgen Klopp named Manager of the Year 2021/22

On stage at the Grosvenor House Hotel in London, the usually ultra-confident Jürgen Klopp for once appeared out of his comfort zone. Dressed in an unfamiliar black suit, shirt and tie that he'd had to buy earlier in the day, he found all eyes focused on him.

Moments earlier, a smiling Sir Alex Ferguson, through gritted teeth but with tongue firmly in cheek, had joked, "This is agony" when announcing Klopp as the 2022 League Managers Association Manager of the Year. Having already been named Premier League Manager of the Year at the same ceremony, Klopp had a double cause for celebration.

Unlike in 2020, when Covid restrictions dictated that the trophies had to be presented unceremoniously behind the closed gates of Liverpool's Melwood training ground, this time Klopp had been invited to attend in person and was therefore now required to deliver an acceptance speech.

Speaking in public, even at large events, was not something that would normally faze Klopp but having to talk about himself brought on a slight sense of uneasiness. Clutching onto one of his awards, he thanked those who had voted for him and reflected briefly on the previous nine months.

"This being voted for by my colleagues is obviously the most important prize you can get," said the Reds boss. "It is a great honour and it was an insane season. It was not the best outcome for us, but we are already over it."

Having insisted his coaching staff accompanied him to the capital, Klopp then pointed to the corner where they were sat and made sure he shared the honour with them. "When you win a prize like this, you are either a genius or you have the best coaching staff in the world – and I am here with all of my coaching staff, they know how much I appreciate them," he added. "I don't believe in individual prizes in football generally. It is a team sport and I would be nothing without these boys there. It is all about what we can do together and what we did together."

Back at the training ground the following morning, he gathered all the players together to extend his gratitude, telling them: "Thank you for making the world believe we are good coaches."

These two prestigious awards were deserved recognition for the huge part he had played in taking Liverpool to within a point of the Premier League title, a place in the Champions League Final, and success in both the League Cup and FA Cup.

Although he would have been too modest to admit as much, it was also further proof, if needed, that in Jürgen Klopp, Liverpool Football Club had themselves one of the best managers in the game.

Next page:
Jürgen catches up with Tom Werner, John Henry and Mike Gordon during a pre-season visit to the US.

"Liverpool is a club steeped in the legacy of legendary managers. Jürgen not only honoured that heritage; he set a new benchmark for those who will follow. His tenure infused the club with a relentless spirit of competitiveness, and it will be marked by the countless trophies the club garnered since 2015. I have been privileged to call Jürgen a close friend, and while football is central, his genuine warmth, sharp wit and embracing nature – along with his humble demeanour – are what stands out to me. I also admire him for his understanding of the importance of life's broader values. His achievements have indeed surpassed our most ambitious expectations!"

TOM WERNER FENWAY SPORTS GROUP AND LIVERPOOL FC CHAIRMAN

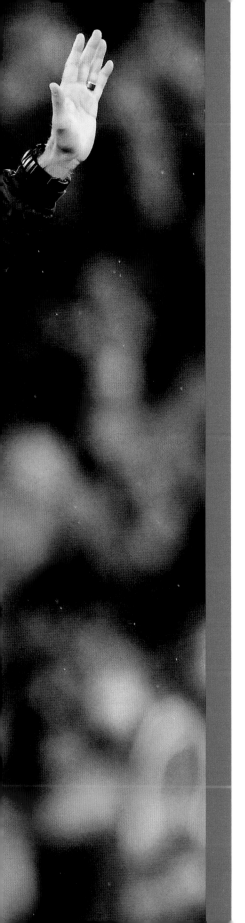

THE LAST DANCE

―――――――

2022–24

"The spotlight was on me when I first joined Liverpool, but the manager put no pressure on me whatsoever, which was great. It was difficult because of the language barrier but he gave me a lot of confidence and told me to just play to my strengths. Like I had done in the Champions League games against Liverpool for Benfica, he said, but just try to be calmer. And then, in one of my first games, I scored to help us win the Community Shield. It's always a lovely feeling to win things so that is a goal I will always remember. In the two years that I played for him, he was a coach who helped me a lot to grow both as a player and as a person. He has taught me many lessons and I take that as a positive for the rest of my career."

DARWIN NUNEZ

VICTORY SHIELD

Liverpool v Manchester City | Community Shield, 30 July 2022

The annual curtain-raiser to the English football season has had its detractors ever since the fixture was first played back in the early 1900s. How seriously it should be treated is debated on a yearly basis and qualifying for it is viewed as more important than actually winning it.

As FA Cup holders, Liverpool had earned the right to compete for the Community Shield against Premier League champions Manchester City. The identity of the opposition meant this year it was perhaps treated more competitively than usual.

While representing one last chance to build up fitness ahead of the new season, it was also a first opportunity to pick up some silverware and lay down an early marker for the months ahead.

On the two previous occasions Klopp's Liverpool had contested this fixture, it had ended in defeat on penalties at Wembley, the first occasion being against City in 2019 and then Arsenal a year later, so the manager was also keen for that balance to be redressed.

"What better way to kick it all off than Liverpool versus Manchester City? This is a fixture that is only ever unbelievably intense and of an incredibly high standard," said Klopp beforehand. "Today is about enjoying what we achieved last season and

Above:
The start of Jürgen's Liverpool 2.0 project as the team line up ahead of the Community Shield.

continuing our preparations for the new one. It's also about looking to win a trophy that I know Liverpool has not won for quite a few years."

With a number of notable departures during the summer, including cult heroes Sadio Mané and Divock Origi, Klopp was in the infancy of a gradual rebuilding process. In terms of new arrivals, the highest-profile signing had been centre-forward Darwin Nunez. The Uruguayan joined for a club-record fee from Benfica and, despite starting on the bench at the Leicester City Stadium, would go on to have a big part to play.

Trent Alexander-Arnold gave Liverpool a deserved half-time lead only for City to equalise midway through the second half. But then Nunez came on, and it wasn't long before he started to make an impact. Seven minutes from time, his header was handled on the line and, from the spot, Mo Salah restored the lead. Then, in the dying moments, he celebrated his debut by scoring the goal that secured victory and Liverpool's first Community Shield success since 2006.

"That goal was obviously the icing on the cake, so I am really pleased for him," said the manager. "You could see in his face; you could see in the face of all his team-mates how happy the boys are for him and that's a really good sign. It was, for me, a really nice watch, especially when you win it in the end. If you win it, it's a very important competition. If you lose it, then it becomes less important."

As Community Shields go, it was one that will live in the memory longer than most, while for Klopp it had been a valuable silver-lined pre-season run out.

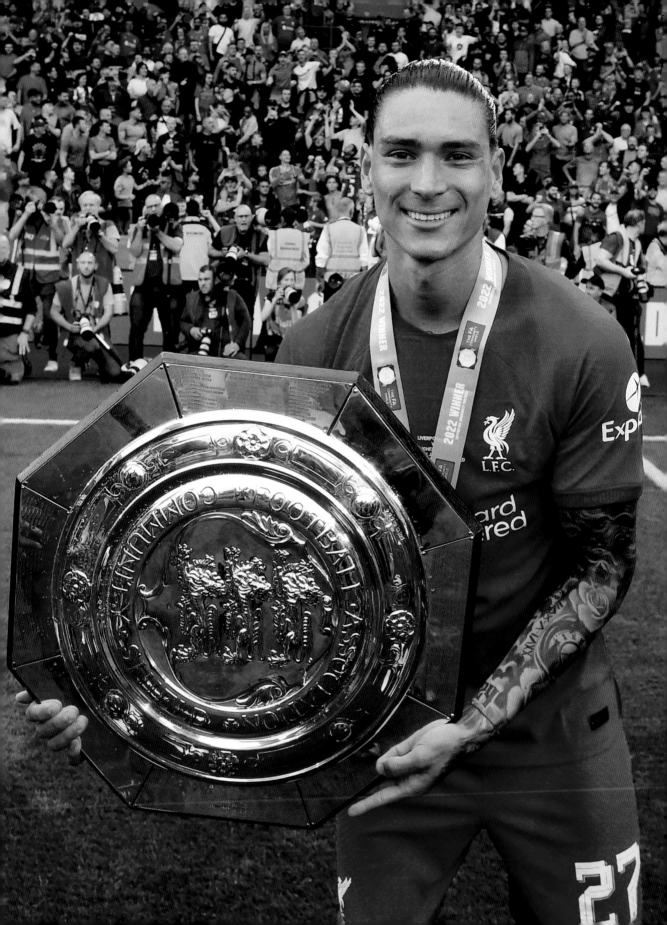

CLOUD NINE

Liverpool v Bournemouth | Premier League, 27 August 2022

When the sun is shining and your team is scoring goals for fun, football really does appear to be the beautiful game, and on what was to be a record-breaking day, this was Jürgen Klopp's Liverpool at their sharp-shooting best.

With two draws and a defeat from their opening three Premier League games in 2022/23, Liverpool's start to the season had not been the best and, given the high standards that had been set, it prompted a typical over-the-top reaction in the media.

Klopp simply brushed this off as nothing other than a "false start". Incredulous claims of a crisis were quickly flattened in the most emphatic manner, with Bournemouth the unfortunate victims on the receiving end of the backlash.

The merciless mauling of The Cherries began after just three minutes and didn't stop until the 85th. "I loved the start today so much," said the manager. "We didn't hesitate, we didn't hold anything back, we just went into the game fully flying and put them under pressure. That's the risk you have to take."

Below left: Luis Diaz celebrates with Jordan Henderson after his 3rd-minute goal starts the rout.

Below right: Fabio Carvalho scores his first goal for the club to make it 8-0.

LIVERPOOL FC   9   16:55
BOURNEMOUTH   0   90:00

Luis Diaz got the ball rolling and Harvey Elliott grabbed his first league goal to quickly double the advantage. Trent Alexander-Arnold, Roberto Firmino and Virgil van Dijk then got on the scoresheet as Liverpool racked up five goals before half-time for the first time in 48 years.

"At half-time it was important for us that we kept it going, because we didn't want to let them score one and have this kind of bitter taste after a wonderful afternoon, so you have to get out of the blocks again," Klopp said.

Within two minutes of the second half, the brutal beating resumed courtesy of an own goal. Firmino then netted his second and Fabio Carvalho celebrated his first goal in a red shirt before Diaz scored again to finally complete the rout and put a shell-shocked Bournemouth out of their misery.

"It was the perfect football afternoon for us, with a lot of different goalscorers, wonderful goals and fantastic situations," concluded Klopp. "We were really on it and put the opponent under incredible pressure. We all know we needed something like that. We had to prove a point for ourselves."

It had been a highly satisfactory and memorable afternoon, and, as the goals flew in, the statisticians in the press box were quickly flicking through the record books to verify the facts.

Not only did the 9-0 scoreline comfortably surpass Liverpool's previous record win in the Premier League era, 7-0 away to Crystal Palace in 2020, it also equalled the club's best ever top-flight victory, against the same opponents in 1989.

The doubters had been silenced and Jürgen Klopp had enjoyed the biggest win yet of his lengthy managerial career.

Above:
The scoreboard says it all, Liverpool's joint-highest top-flight victory.

Next page:
Harvey Elliott celebrates after scoring his first Premier League goal during the 9-0 rout of Bournemouth.

"To score my first Premier League goal was a dream come true but to do so for a team managed by Jürgen Klopp made it even more special because I didn't just play for the badge, I played for him. He's a manager who I would always run myself into the ground for. That goal came at a tough time personally. My nan passed away a few days before, but I kept the news to myself until afterwards. When the manager found out, he was straight over with a massive hug and to say he was there for me. It summed him up. On and off the pitch he always had our back and without him I wouldn't be where I am today. He's a Liverpool icon who created so many amazing experiences for players and supporters. For me, there'll never be another Jürgen Klopp."

HARVEY ELLIOTT

MR LIVERPOOL

Jürgen Klopp awarded the Freedom of Liverpool, 2 November 2022

From the moment he first walked through the gates of Anfield in 2015, Jürgen Klopp displayed all the traits that Liverpudlians love so much in a manager. Titles and trophies obviously help, but the strength of the relationship Klopp developed with fans was formed by how he acted off the pitch as much as how his team performed on it.

From his continuous support for the victims of the Hillsborough disaster, to visiting sick children in local hospitals and regularly taking time out to pose for photographs with supporters, Klopp captured the hearts of many.

In their eyes, the bearded guy from the Black Forest in Germany has always been 'one of their own' and, while his accent remained more Swabian than Scouse, he proved on countless occasions that he was clearly a man in tune with the people of this city.

It was therefore only fitting that in the autumn of 2022, Klopp became an honorary Scouser when awarded the Freedom of the City of Liverpool, in acknowledgement of his achievements at Anfield and his contributions to numerous local charities.

The city's highest civic honour had previously only been bestowed on three footballing figures – Bob Paisley, Sir Kenny Dalglish and Steven Gerrard – while other notable freemen of the city include the Beatles, Gerry Marsden, Ken Dodd and the 97 victims of the Hillsborough disaster.

Klopp became only the third foreign national to be given the honour and admitted he was overwhelmed to be recognised alongside so many luminaries. "For a city we love so much, getting something like this really is big," he said.

Speaking at a special ceremony in Liverpool Town Hall, where he received his prestigious scroll alongside wife Ulla, the Reds boss added: "Over the years you realise that the Scouse people and us as a family have a lot of things in common. We care about similar things, have similar political views and we like to be very open. That's how it is. All people around me, my friends and family, see more of the city than I do and I hear always that they enjoy it exactly because of that; because people are really open, nice, kind and friendly. That's what I want to be as well.

"I have to be honest, when I first heard this news, I had to take a minute to take it in. As you can imagine, this was definitely a 'wow' moment. The main reason for this was what Liverpool, the city and its wonderful people, mean to

me and my family. The welcome that we have been given has been unbelievable from the word go, so to get this kind of recognition is incredible. It is also very humbling.

"So, to everyone who made this possible – thank you. You have made my family and myself so, so proud to know that the bond we have with this wonderful city has been made even stronger and will now stay forever."

In the words of the flag that has been displayed on the Kop since his first season at the club…'Jürgen Norbert Klopp. Boss Tha'.

Above: Jürgen is granted the Freedom of the City in a ceremony at Liverpool Town Hall.

Next page: In receiving the award he follows in some illustrious footsteps.

"From day one with Jürgen, expectations were high. We all wondered what he'd deliver, and in the words of the song, he delivered what he said. He brought us a multitude of cups and a different style of football to what we'd been used to, wonderful attacking football that'll be remembered for decades. He gave us so much enjoyment and good vibes. To be given the Freedom of Liverpool was deserved. As a foreigner coming into this country, it's such an unbelievable honour and it's not just for the trophies he's won. It's from the people of this city and that makes it even more special. Being the proud Scouser that I am, I'd say it's akin to getting a knighthood and I look forward to seeing him guide his cattle through the streets in years to come. For what he's achieved here, Jürgen will always have our extreme appreciation."

PHIL THOMPSON

THROWN TO THE WOLVES

Wolves v Liverpool, Premier League, 4 February 2023

Although Jürgen Klopp could do no wrong in the eyes of Liverpool supporters, he wasn't exempt from criticism. As a season of promise tumbled towards a huge anti-climax, he found himself in the firing line.

After coming so close to an unprecedented quadruple in the previous campaign, hopes had been high at Anfield, especially after defeating Manchester City to lift the Community Shield. The emphatic victory over Bournemouth in August 2022 was not an isolated incident either; other big wins followed, notably winning 7-1 away to Rangers in the Champions League, but inconsistency would plague them.

Alarm bells had started to ring when struggling Leeds United had won at Merseyside in late October. It left Liverpool eight points adrift of the top four. Even at this early stage in the campaign, Klopp acknowledged his team were in trouble. "You can't qualify for the Champions League if you play as inconsistently as we do at the moment," he said.

As Christmas approached, their defence of the League Cup was brought to an abrupt halt in the fourth round by Manchester City, and a month later they relinquished their grip on the FA Cup at the same stage, losing away to Brighton & Hove Albion.

In Europe, Klopp had, yet again, managed to take Liverpool through to the knockout phase of the Champions League but, by early February, it was looking

Below left:
Stefan Bajcetic in aerial combat with Matheus Cunha at Molineux.

Below right:
Trent Alexander-Arnold can't bear to look as the Reds slip to a heavy defeat.

increasingly likely that to be back in that competition next year, they would have to win it.

Six defeats in the Premier League had raised serious doubts about Liverpool's credentials to finish in the top four. At Molineux on the first weekend of the month, their season sank to a new low. Against Wolves, another side fighting relegation, the Reds conceded twice within the first 12 minutes and registered just one shot on target during a first half to forget.

Even with a front three of Mo Salah, Darwin Nunez and the Netherlands' World Cup star Cody Gakpo, who had signed from PSV Eindhoven during the recent January transfer window, they were unable to hit back, and Wolves added to the agony with a third goal after the break.

Liverpool had slumped to tenth in the table and an apologetic Klopp was almost lost for words. "I have no explanation, I'm sorry," he said afterwards, visibly shell-shocked by what he had just witnessed. "You can criticise and judge us, and you are probably right. We caused the misery. It cannot happen and it needs to change."

For the first time in over a decade, Liverpool had now lost three successive away games in the Premier League, and they were suffering a crisis of confidence, particularly in defence. Wolves supporters taunted Klopp with laughable chants of 'you're getting sacked in the morning'.

As they often do, the media overhyped the moment and Liverpool's rivals revelled in it, but there could be no disguising the fact that the manager had a big job on his hands to turn things around. When asked if he was confident of doing so, Jürgen Klopp replied: "Yes. Absolutely."

Above: Harvey Elliott comes on to replace Stefan Bajcetic but it failed to inspire a comeback.

Next page: Spanish mid-fielder Stefan Bajcetic, another youngster given a chance to impress by Jürgen.

"He gave me, and a lot of other young players, the opportunity to show ourselves to the world. Since day one, the manager and his coaching staff were nothing but supportive, and I'm very thankful for that. As a young player coming through the ranks, it makes you feel so good, and to be part of Jürgen Klopp's first team was something I had been dreaming of since I joined the club. From playing under-18s football to making my senior debut and scoring my first goal, it all happened so fast. He has been such a big influence on my career so far, allowing me to play with the freedom and confidence that enabled me to make an impression and improve as a player. I'll always be grateful to him for having that faith in me."

STEFAN BAJCETIC

THE MAGNIFICENT SEVEN

Liverpool v Manchester United | Premier League, 5 March 2023

Sometimes in football you just have to sit back and appreciate what is unfolding before your eyes: an unprecedented scenario that may never happen again, a moment where the stars align, and everything just falls into place.

On the first weekend of March 2023, Liverpool supporters were privileged to experience exactly this, as Jürgen Klopp's team treated them to a performance and end result that scaled previously unchartered heights against a club they love to beat more than most.

No-one believed Liverpool's famous 5-0 rout of Manchester United at Old Trafford in October 2021 could be topped. But just when the Mancunians thought it couldn't get any worse, Klopp and his players contrived to prove otherwise.

Although United had not recorded a win in front of the Kop since three months into Klopp's reign in January 2016, and had suffered a 4-0 loss on their last visit here, Erik ten Hag's side went into this game as the team in form, 10 points ahead of Liverpool in the table. What followed made a mockery of that, even if the first half was a much closer contest than the eventual scoreline would suggest.

It took until just before half-time for the hosts to break the deadlock through Cody Gakpo. But by the 50th minute, following quickfire goals from Darwin Nunez and Gakpo again, the three points were virtually secured. "The second half could not have started better. From that moment on the boys were flying and it was really difficult to play against us," said Klopp.

Mo Salah, so often United's chief tormentor, then got in on the act, netting twice to become the club's all-time leading Premier League goalscorer. Sandwiched in

Below left:
Cody Gakpo celebrates after opening the scoring against Manchester United.

Below right:
He then repeats the feat in the second half after netting another.

between Salah's double was another strike by Nunez as the rampant Reds turned on the style.

With a joyous home crowd revelling in the misery Klopp's men were inflicting on their age-old rivals, journalists frantically searched for new superlatives to describe what they were witnessing. And there was still time for more shame to be heaped on the dispirited visitors.

Not content with six, Liverpool proceeded to rub further salt into United's open wounds. During the final few minutes, it was the soon to be departing Roberto Firmino who applied the sweetest of icing to the cake, coming off the bench to complete an unprecedented 7-0 annihilation.

Not only was it a record victory for this fixture, surpassing Liverpool's 7-1 win way back in 1895, it was also United's joint-heaviest defeat, and when delivering his post-match verdict, Klopp was left in awe of just how well Liverpool had played. "Spectacular football game, outstanding. We played top football against the team in form. One of the best performances for a long, long time."

No Liverpool manager had enjoyed more emphatic success over Manchester United than Jürgen Klopp did and there have been very few, if indeed any, more enjoyable afternoons at Anfield. It was one that Liverpudlians will never tire of remembering.

"I was very excited to come here and work under such a great manager. He helped me develop and become a better player. The Manchester United game is an obvious highlight. To play a part in that was amazing. He told me beforehand how big a fixture it was and put his trust in me, so to repay him by scoring twice on what turned out to be such a historic afternoon is something I will never forget. When I came off in the second half, I remember him telling me how pleased he had been with my performance and that meant a lot. What he did for this club was amazing. He was constantly thinking ahead and giving us belief that we could succeed, even in the tough times. I'll always be grateful to him for giving me the opportunity to play for this beautiful club."

CODY GAKPO

HEROES AND VILLAINS

Liverpool v Aston Villa | Premier League, 20 May 2023

A week after Liverpool dished out that famous seven-goal hiding to Manchester United, they lost 1-0 away to Bournemouth. It summed up the erratic nature of their campaign in a nutshell. Within 10 days, Real Madrid had also ended their interest in the Champions League. Just like they had been in 2020/21, Jürgen Klopp and his team were left relying on a top-four finish to save the season.

Fans were justifiably nervous, but from early April to early May, it had looked as though a light had suddenly been switched on. Liverpool strung together an impressive seven-game winning run, the highlights of which included two more high-scoring victories that featured seven goals, 6-1 away to Leeds and 4-3 at home to Tottenham, the latter being particularly memorable for its Diogo Jota stoppage-time winner.

They had gained ground on Newcastle United and Manchester United, third and fourth in the table respectively, but as it came to the final games of the season, for Liverpool to secure their place, they required one of them to falter.

Below:
Curtis Jones in possession during the final home game of the 2022/23 campaign.

Of course, the Reds also had to keep their side of the bargain, by maintaining their winning streak, and the pivotal moment came on the penultimate weekend of the league season, when they played host to Aston Villa.

It had just been announced that several key players would be leaving in the summer, so an emotional and highly charged occasion was always guaranteed. The manager, meanwhile, was looking to the future and planning a major rebuild of his team.

Villa took the sting out of the occasion by taking a first-half lead. The game needed the intervention of departing fans' favourite Roberto Firmino to lift the mood. The Brazilian, one of four players the Kop was bidding farewell to, came off the bench midway through the half to mark his final Anfield appearance by grabbing an equaliser in the final minute. It was a touching moment and one that provided a glimmer of hope for qualification. In reality, though, a point was never going to be enough.

Liverpool's top-four chances were left hanging by the slimmest of threads. Their fate was finally sealed a few days later by results elsewhere. It was the first time since the manager's inaugural season at the club that they had finished outside the Premier League's top four and Klopp was the first to acknowledge that it had been a case of too little too late. "I think we made it pretty exciting. I didn't think that was possible seven weeks ago. The boys did really well in that period, [but] we were for too long not good enough or ourselves," he said.

With James Milner, Naby Keita and Alex Oxlade-Chamberlain joining Firmino on the way out, it seemed like the end of an era. But with Liverpool about to enter a phase of transition, Jürgen Klopp defiantly vowed: "We will be a contender again."

Above left:
Roberto Firmino's goal rescued a point for Liverpool on what was his last-ever Anfield appearance.

Above right:
No player made more appearances for the club under Jürgen than Firmino.

Next page:
Reds legend Steven Gerrard admits he would have loved to play for Jürgen's Liverpool.

"After the first interview he gave as Liverpool manager you're almost shadow boxing in the mirror. It was 'game on'. I remember then playing for the club in an exhibition match, Jürgen took the team and it left me thinking, 'I would pay any amount of money, and I would do anything for anyone, if I could represent this guy for one year.' Before he arrived, there had been a lot of pain, a lot of hurt and a lot of doubt, but he improved players and built winning sides that were brilliant to watch. This job comes with huge pressure. We've had the likes of Shankly, Paisley, Fagan, Benitez … managers who delivered the big prizes for Liverpool, but Jürgen, for what he's achieved, is right up there, alongside the best, for sure. I just hope there's a statue in the making because he deserves that recognition at the club."

STEVEN GERRARD

JOY ON THE TYNE

Newcastle v Liverpool | Premier League, 27 August 2023

Liverpool could have been forgiven for installing a revolving door at the entrance to their training ground during the summer of 2023 as Jürgen Klopp set about the reconstruction of his team and, in particular, the midfield. He dubbed the project 'Liverpool 2.0' and hoped it would signal the start of another glorious new chapter in his story at the club.

Following a season in which the Reds had finished trophyless and failed to qualify for the Champions League, an overhaul of playing personnel was always likely but the departure of so many figures who had played a key role in the success between 2019 and 2022 made it even an even bigger job.

While it was known in advance that Roberto Firmino, James Milner, Naby Keita and Alex Oxlade-Chamberlain would be leaving, a parting of the ways with Fabinho and captain Jordan Henderson had not been anticipated.

Below:
Young defender Jarell Quansah impresses with an accomplished performance on his Premier League debut.

"I'll never forget what he's done for me and my career. He gave me the opportunity to play in the first team at the football club I've always wanted to play for. More importantly, he showed so much trust and belief in me. The game at Newcastle when I made my debut really stands out. To throw on a young centre-back who had never played in the Premier League before would be frowned upon by some, so for him to just do it without hesitation was an unbelievable feeling and it gave me so much confidence. He didn't say much in that moment but knowing he had faith in me was all I needed. It's a shame we didn't get to work together for longer but even in the short space of time that I was in his team, I gained so much knowledge from him."

JARELL QUANSAH

Above left: It's tense on the touchline as Jürgen reacts to Virgil van Dijk's sending off.

Above right: Darwin Nunez came off the bench to snatch the points with two late goals.

Opposite: The Uruguayan runs to the corner to celebrate in front of the travelling Liverpudlians.

Klopp sought to fill the gaping midfield void by bringing in the highly rated Hungary captain Dominik Szoboszlai, World Cup winner Alexis Mac Allister, Ryan Gravenberch from Bayern Munich and the lesser-known Wataru Endo. Alongside his existing core of players, and with a clutch of exciting youngsters waiting in the wings, he believed the squad was well-equipped to challenge once again.

"It was the job we had to do, and this summer was a moment for that," the manager explained. "I was really excited about the rebuild, the new way, the new energy. We decided last year we had to change a lot. But we wanted to change it for good, not because we have to. I loved everything about the seven years before but obviously we all need energy sources and looking at these faces every day to see how much they enjoy the new challenge gives me energy as well."

The re-energised Reds made an instant impression in the 2023/24 season, winning all but one of the opening eight games and proving their mettle in a thrilling late August win at Newcastle. With three of the new faces involved, Liverpool fought back from the blow of conceding first and then losing new captain Virgil van Dijk to a red card, both before the half-hour mark.

In the 77th minute, with hopes fading fast and frustration rising, Klopp made a double substitution, sending on young defender Jarell Quansah for his debut along with Darwin Nunez. Within four minutes Nunez drew Liverpool level, then in stoppage time he pounced again to complete a remarkable turnaround.

"We have new key players in the team and we have to create key moments and this was definitely a key moment," enthused the boss afterwards. "I think in my 1,000 games as a coach or a manager I never had a game like this, 10 men in an atmosphere like this against an opponent like this. It was super-special and the boys deserved it."

To snatch all three points off a side that had edged them out of the top four the previous season was hugely important for Jürgen Klopp's revamped Liverpool, and a positive sign for the future.

BOMBSHELL

Jürgen Klopp's departure announcement, 26 January 2024

Nothing lasts forever and all good things must eventually come to an end, but nobody was prepared for this… Not just yet anyway. After eight and a half unforgettable years of Jürgen Klopp at Liverpool, it was hoped there would be at least a few more. And then came the unforeseen revelation that would change everything.

It was a routine Friday morning on Merseyside, the sun was shining and there was plenty to be positive about. Plans were being made for another trip to Wembley, after Klopp had guided Liverpool to an aggregate victory over Fulham in the League Cup semi-final just two nights earlier, while preparations were underway for the weekend's FA Cup fourth-round tie at home to Norwich City. Added to that, the Reds were five points clear at the top of the Premier League and still in Europe.

There was no indication whatsoever that a dark cloud loomed. At the club's first-team headquarters in Kirkby, the players reported for training as normal, only to be summoned to a meeting where the manager informed them of the shock news that was about to break.

It was shortly after 10:30am and it coincided with the publication of a carefully planned statement that was released via the club's official website and social media channels, alongside a video message that had been quickly pre-recorded just hours earlier. The headline simply read, 'Jürgen Klopp announces decision to step down as Liverpool manager at the end of the season'.

The seismic ramifications of those 16 words would reverberate around the world within a matter of seconds. At first, supporters hoped, believed and prayed that it was some sort of prank, that the website had been hacked or April Fools' Day had come early.

To say people were stunned would be a massive understatement. The magnitude of the announcement was so huge, it was difficult to comprehend. Out on the streets and in offices, factories and schools, everything came to a temporary standstill, and everyone asked the same question: why?

"I can understand that it's a shock for a lot of people in this moment, when you hear it for the first time, but obviously I can explain it – or at least try to explain it," said Klopp as he began to outline his reasons for deciding to step down. "I love absolutely everything about this club, I love everything about the city, I love everything about our supporters, I love the team, I love the staff. I love everything. But that I still take this decision shows you that I am convinced it is the one I have to take.

"When I heard the decision, of course I was disappointed, both professionally and personally. But as Jürgen and I discussed his choice to leave the club at the end of the season, it was clear it was absolutely the right decision for him, his family and, by extension, for the club. I could see it in his eyes. He was totally at peace with the decision. There was no lingering doubt, no 'maybe' … and so the discussion turned to how we communicate this in the best possible way. Jürgen's ability to speak authentically, directly and with empathy has made him beloved. His leadership has brought us success on and off the pitch, leaving us all with incredible memories and unbelievable emotional highs. I will truly miss him as a friend and colleague – and I speak for everyone when I say we wish him and his family nothing but the best. Thank you, Jürgen. YNWA.

BILLY HOGAN LIVERPOOL FC
CHIEF EXECUTIVE OFFICER

"I am running out of energy. I know that I cannot do the job again and again and again and again. After the years we had together and after all the time we spent together and after all the things we went through together, the respect grew for you, the love grew for you and the least I owe you is the truth – and that is the truth."

Klopp insisted it wasn't a decision made in haste and revealed that he'd informed the club of his intentions three months before. "I told the club in November. A season starts and you plan pretty much the next season already. When we sat there together talking about potential signings, the next summer camp and can we go wherever, the thought came up, 'I am not sure I am here then any more' and I was surprised myself by that. I obviously started thinking about it."

To the outside world, the timing just still didn't make sense. Klopp was in the process of building his second great Anfield team. His recent recruits had settled well, plus he had a clutch of exciting youngsters waiting in the wings. Much to his own surprise, 'Liverpool 2.0', as he labelled it, was gelling quicker than expected and with the team suddenly competing strongly on all four fronts once again, the project appeared to be well on track, if not already ahead of schedule.

"Last season [2022/23] was kind of a super-difficult season," he continued to explain, "and there were moments when at other clubs probably the decision would have been, 'Come on, thank you very much for everything but probably we should split here, or end it here.' That didn't happen here, obviously. For me it was super, super, super-important that I can help to bring this team back onto the rails.

"It was all I was thinking about. When I realised pretty early that happened, it's a really good team with massive potential and a super age group, super characters and all that, then I could start thinking about myself again and that was the outcome. It is not what I want to [do], it is just what I think is 100 per cent right. That's it."

Klopp was also quick to allay fears that the news could have an adverse effect on the players in the middle of a season that was shaping into something special. "The boys are in a really good mood. It was not that they were getting up and having a party when I told them but it was just an announcement," he added. "There were some tears but that's normal after such a long time together.

"In an ideal world I wouldn't have said anything to anybody until the end of the season. In the world we are living in, it's not possible to keep things like this secret; it's maybe a surprise that we could keep it [a secret] until now. One thing I am really convinced of [is] if you have to make a decision like that, it is better you do it slightly early than slightly too late. Too late would have been absolutely the worst thing to happen.

"The club needs to know early and needs to plan. Everything we built in the last years is a wonderful platform, a wonderful basis for the future, and the only thing

Next page:
Jürgen stunned the football world when he announced he'd be stepping down as Liverpool manager at the end of the 2023/24 season.

that could disturb that now is pretty much that you cannot make the right decisions because you are running out of time, and that's what was very important to me. This team is set up for the future. When I said Liverpool 2.0, that didn't include me for the next 10 years but the base is there."

For Liverpudlians of a certain vintage, the shock news that Klopp's time at the club would soon be over echoed the departure announcements of Bill Shankly and Kenny Dalglish, two other much-loved former managers, who stepped down in 1974 and 1991 respectively. This was Liverpool's third major 'JFK' moment and its impact, in terms of the initial sheer disbelief and subsequent outpouring of emotion, was very much on a similar scale.

As tributes began to flood in, Klopp was determined that life at Liverpool would continue to operate as normally as possible and by early afternoon he was pictured back out on the training pitch as his players were put through their paces ahead of the weekend fixture. Then he had to face the media at a press conference alongside Liverpool CEO Billy Hogan. Smiling, yet slightly subdued, the boss admitted it was a day of mixed emotions but politely and patiently answered all questions that came his way.

"I still think it is the right thing to do. I don't take these things lightly," he reiterated. "With all the responsibility you have at this club, you have to be at the top of your game. We are not young rabbits any more and we do not jump as high as we did. This club, especially with the team we have, needs a manager on his top game, and when I cannot be that, I have to tell people. I told first the club and then the coaches and then today everyone knows it. The two important things I had to do was to tell our supporters and to tell the players. The relief was there when I made the decision for myself. Today, it's mixed. I'm not as emotional as I will be when it finally comes to an end."

It had been an unexpected but monumental day in the club's history and while the news had come too late for this to be reflected in the weekend's matchday programme, ahead of the following game, the manager reinforced the point that he still had a job to finish here. "My foot is still very much on the gas and it will be until the final minute of my final game. In the way they have acted, spoken and, most importantly, trained and played, the players are in exactly the same mindset so, as I've said, nothing changes. Our ambitions, standards and beliefs are no different. We know what we want and we know how hard we will have to work to achieve it. I, and we, could not be more in this season."

Football in England and, obviously, life at Liverpool were never going to be the same again but there were still four months of Jürgen Klopp to savour and, for now, he didn't want any more talk of his impending departure to get in the way of that.

KLOPP'S KIDS (2)

Liverpool v Chelsea | League Cup Final, 25 February 2024

"You win nothing with kids" is a famous quote attributed to Liverpool legend and serial trophy-winner Alan Hansen. The former defender turned pundit was highly respected for his views on the game, but three decades later Jürgen Klopp was about to put Hansen's theory to the ultimate test.

It had been a month since Klopp shocked the Kop to its core with the announcement that he would be departing come the end of the season but, with just one defeat in the six games, his so-called 'farewell tour' had begun positively. The target was to sign off on a high by delivering more silverware, and the League Cup Final represented the first of four potential opportunities to do so.

Liverpool's run to the final had been a fairly straightforward one, with Leicester City, Bournemouth, West Ham United and Fulham all defeated along the way, and, for the third time, it was Chelsea who would provide the opposition at Wembley.

An encouraging aspect of the previous rounds had been how the manager had utilised his squad to maximum effect. A total of 24 players had been called up in those five games, providing a valuable pathway into the first-team set-up for a number of youngsters. For the final, he would be forced to delve even deeper into the youth ranks.

With at least six regular first-team players ruled out through injury, Klopp's squad was severely depleted for the trip south, meaning young Northern Ireland full-back Conor Bradley started. Bradley had proved himself a more than able deputy for the sidelined Trent Alexander-Arnold, featuring regularly in the side during the past two months, but not in a game of this magnitude. Making up the numbers on the bench were several of his fellow Academy graduates and senior experience among these was severely limited, with two yet to make their debut.

"There are different opportunities to write history, because obviously Liverpool fans never forget," said Klopp ahead of the final. "And yes, a lot of kids played a lot of minutes, which is really, really important for them. Whichever competition, it's a big step for the young players."

Liverpool's injury problems worsened after 25 minutes when Ryan Gravenberch was stretchered off following a challenge by Moises Caicedo. Ex-Red Raheem Sterling then had the ball in the net for Chelsea, only for it to be ruled out for offside, and Liverpool suffered the same fate just before the hour mark when VAR judged Wataru Endo to be fractionally offside in the build-up to Virgil van Dijk heading home from a free-kick.

The match was following a similar pattern to the recent cup finals between these teams in 2022, with both goalkeepers pulling off impressive saves and the woodwork coming to the rescue at either end.

As the afternoon wore on and legs began to tire, Klopp had no option, but also no qualms, about turning to his bench and sending some of the young lads into battle. "The boys have trained for a long time with us. They know exactly what we have to do," he said. "We needed fresh legs. They were fresh but very young, but they did the job." First up was Bobby Clark, midway through the second half, followed by James McConnell and Jayden Danns just before the end of 90 minutes, then Jarell Quansah in extra time.

The Liverpool XI that ended the game included three teenagers and two more aged 21 or under. It was the most inexperienced team the club had ever fielded in a cup final, but it never showed. With the vociferous travelling Kop spurring them on, the young Reds rose to the occasion, refusing to play it safe by sitting back and waiting for penalties. Given the circumstances, that in itself would have been a great achievement, but both their efforts and the manager's faith in them were to be rewarded in a dramatic late twist.

With just two minutes remaining and yet another dreaded shoot-out seemingly on the cards, Liverpool forced a corner. It was fired in from the right by Kostas Tsimikas and, just as he had done earlier in the day, Van Dijk won the aerial challenge to send the ball spinning gloriously into the far corner. This time there was no doubt. The goal stood and ecstatic scenes erupted.

Liverpool had extended their record-breaking run of League Cup wins to 10 and, in a fitting finale to what would be his last appearance at Wembley in this role, Klopp accepted the request from his match-winning captain to get involved with the trophy-lifting duties, emulating Bob Paisley, who did likewise in 1983.

Above left:
Jürgen looks on proudly as the Klopp kids beat Chelsea at Wembley.

Above right:
Young Northern Ireland full-back Conor Bradley with fellow Academy graduates.

"In more than 20 years it is easily the most special trophy I have ever won," said the boss. "What I saw today is so exceptional, it might not happen again. Not because I am on the sidelines but because these things don't happen in football. I got told outside there is a saying in English football: you don't win trophies with kids. I didn't know that. Yeah? Seeing the faces of the kids after the game… Can you create football stories which nobody will forget? It's so difficult. If you find the same story with Academy players coming on against a top side and still winning it, I've never heard of it.

"I was proud of our people for the way they pushed us. I was proud of the staff for creating this kind of atmosphere where these boys can just do what they are best at. I was proud of our Academy. I was proud of my coaches. I was proud of so many things. It was really overwhelming. We had problems before the game and they became bigger during the game. Getting through all those things makes this a night I will never forget. It's a really nice memory forever."

Excluding the Community Shield, this was the seventh major honour of Jürgen Klopp's Anfield career, elevating him to joint second on the list of Liverpool's most decorated managers. No previous senior trophy in the club's history had been won with a team containing so many young players though.

On the flight home later that night the soon-to-be-departing manager slept with the cup in his arms, content in the knowledge that the kids he'd be leaving behind had just come of age.

Below: Jarell Quansah, Conor Bradley and Harvey Elliott with the League Cup.

"It was an incredible feeling for everyone but especially us younger lads. It wasn't easy with all the injuries, but the gaffer had faith in us and knowing that meant so much. For me, it doesn't get much bigger than playing for Liverpool in a cup final at Wembley but he made sure the size of the occasion didn't get to us. His approach was always the same. 'Just be confident, enjoy it and play your normal game,' he said. Getting the win was a reward for the confidence he instilled in us. He means everything to me. He gave me my first break at this club and has been so important in my development as a footballer. He is just so inspirational, and what he has done for the club as a whole has been amazing. I'm just so thankful for everything he has done for me."

CONOR BRADLEY

THE FINAL FAREWELL

Liverpool v Wolves | Premier League, 19 May 2024

It was the day everyone had been dreading since Jürgen Klopp announced he would be calling time on his tenure as Liverpool manager. This was the final stop on an incredible journey and there wasn't a dry eye in house.

As send-offs go, it was the most emotional ever witnessed at Anfield and more than fitting for a man who will forever hold a special place in the hearts of every Liverpudlian.

The dream scenario, of course, would have been for Klopp to bow out lifting the Premier League trophy in front of a packed Kop before hopping over the Irish Sea three nights later to collect the Europa League, the only trophy needed to complete his set. Sadly that wasn't to be, but not even that could spoil an occasion and spectacle that overshadowed almost everything else happening in the sporting world that day.

After winning the League Cup, there had been genuine talk, once again, of a quadruple. Unfortunately, it was short lived. Interest in the FA Cup was cruelly curtailed in the dying moments of a thrilling quarter-final against Manchester United at Old Trafford. It was a game Liverpool should have won easily and the defeat hurt immensely.

The psychological scars took time to heal, and it ultimately derailed their campaign. Atalanta then came to Anfield and unexpectedly dashed hopes of a trip to Dublin with an emphatic victory. Overturning a 3-0 deficit was certainly not beyond the realms of fantasy for a Jürgen Klopp side but on this occasion it wasn't to be, and the Reds exited tamely.

That left Liverpool with just the Premier League to focus on. They had played their part in what was developing into a closely contested three-horse title race with Arsenal and Manchester City, but with the final straight in sight, damaging defeats at home to Crystal Palace and away to Everton allowed the other two to pull clear.

The team were clearly running low on energy and the season petered out. Questions were asked about the timing of Klopp's announcement in January and whether this had adversely affected the players. The reality of the situation, though, was that this was still very much a team in transition. To win a trophy and comfortably secure Champions League qualification was a more than commendable return, one that offered positive signs for the future.

Klopp's impending departure and Liverpool's drop-off in form obviously cast a shadow over the final months of the season, but as the final weekend approached,

Above:
Jürgen leads
his coaching
staff in saluting
supporters on
the Kop one
final time.

thoughts turned to how lucky we had had been to experience nine years of a manager who totally transformed the club's fortunes. As supporters reminisced about the good times and a multitude of touching tributes flooded social media, smiles returned to faces, while parties were planned to celebrate his achievements and give him the send-off he deserved.

The clamour for tickets to be at Anfield for Klopp's final game in charge, against Wolves, was almost unprecedented, even though the result was of little consequence and there was nothing to play for but pride. Liverpool would finish third in the table no matter what but there was a buzz of anticipation on the day that could only have been topped if the destiny of Premier League title had been at stake.

Klopp meant so much to these supporters and they came to show their appreciation. The words of the soundtrack that accompanied the club's official goodbye video summed up the sentiments of the fanbase beautifully: 'You To Me Are Everything'. The way he had managed the club, connected with the fans and embraced life in the city ensured the adulation for him was Shankly-esque. No Liverpool manager since the legendary Scot had come close to being hero-worshipped on such a scale and nobody could begrudge him this emotional final farewell.

Professional to the last, Klopp typically tried to play down the significance of the occasion in his pre-match previews and reiterated the point in his final ever

matchday programme notes. "First and foremost – in fact first, second and last – Sunday is a matchday," he wrote. "We cannot and will not lose sight of that. Since I have been here there have been many, many games where other things have been happening but the absolute rule is that from the first whistle to the final whistle, we do everything we can to play proper Liverpool football. After that, we can enjoy the occasion, but business always has to come first and always has to be the priority."

He was 100 per cent correct, but in reality, the action on the pitch really didn't matter. Nor did what was happening elsewhere in the Premier League that afternoon. Prior to kick-off, a carnival atmosphere engulfed the streets around Anfield. Inside the ground, a mosaic on three sides of the stadium paid tribute to the departing boss, spelling out the words 'Danke Jürgen YNWA', and flags in his honour were waved proudly on the Kop, a standout one being 'Doubters, Believers, Conquerors'.

Throughout the game, supporters sang Klopp's name loud and proud, while also dipping into their extensive back catalogue to remember the players who had played such a key part in the manager's amazing journey with the club. As game drew to a close, it was Klopp's song that boomed out, almost incessantly, once again. A 2-0 win for the Reds was an apt way to finish an Anfield managerial reign that exceeded expectations and yielded a collection of silverware that most clubs can only look on with envy. For the majority of the 61,000 members of the crowd, the final whistle couldn't come fast enough because then they could really pay homage to the man who had made their dreams come true, the longest-serving and most successful Liverpool manager since Bob Paisley.

After tributes had been paid to the players and coaches who were also leaving, Klopp was welcomed back onto the pitch for the final time, his team forming a guard of honour as he emerged from the tunnel amid a deafening crescendo of

"Jürgen's tenure in Liverpool was nothing short of transformative. He was instrumental in bringing about one of the club's most successful eras by embodying that rare leadership quality that inspired loyalty and dedication. He didn't just lead; he created a magnetic force that drew people in and made them continually strive to be better. Jürgen immediately embraced our expectations for the club and also arrived understanding the bond between the team, its supporters and the city of Liverpool. It was a major factor in his decision to take the reins. It takes a truly remarkable individual to command the respect and admiration of Anfield's discerning fans. It was clear in sending his fist through the air at the end of so many important victories that he perfectly matched the love, the enthusiasm and emotion of the Kop and our supporters worldwide."

JOHN W HENRY PRINCIPAL OWNER, FENWAY SPORTS GROUP

Above:
The Liverpool players form a guard of honour as Jürgen walks out at Anfield for the last time.

Opposite and next page:
As Jürgen said his final goodbyes on an emotional Anfield afternoon, many tears were openly shed.

applause. As he made his way to the specially assembled stage, his name was chanted loudly once more. Then, the ground fell silent, as Klopp took hold of the microphone to deliver his eagerly anticipated farewell speech. "I'm completely surprised. I thought, 'I'm already in pieces,' to be honest, but I'm not. I'm so happy, I can't believe it," he said. "I'm so happy about you all, about the atmosphere, about the game, about being part of this family, about us, how we celebrated this day. It's just incredible. Thank you so much."

With the crowd hanging on his every word, he continued: "People told me that I turned them from doubters to believers. That's not true. Believing is an active act: you have to do it yourself. I just said we have to. You did it. That's a big difference. And nobody tells you now to stop believing. Because this club is in a better moment than ever. Maybe ever – I have to ask Kenny [Dalglish]! Since a long time, let me say it like that. We have this wonderful stadium, we have this wonderful training centre. We have you – the superpower of world football. Wow. I'm one of you now. I love you to bits. On my jumper is 'Thank you Luv' and 'I will never walk alone again'. Thank you for that! You are the best people in the world. Thank you!"

After exiting the stage to another rousing roar, it was time to carry out one more act. On cue, he treated the fans in all four stands to his legendary fist pumps for the last time. The cheers, the applause and the songs continued, while the tears also flowed as the final curtain came down on a glorious, never-to-be forgotten Anfield era.

Eight years, seven months and 11 days. 491 games, 1,035 goals and 299 victories. Eight trophies and memories that will last a lifetime.

Jürgen Klopp, King of the Kop, we salute you.

Thank you to all the past and present players, coaches and managers who paid tribute to Jürgen, and to those who helped facilitate the interviews that form this book.

BIBLIOGRAPHY

Klopp: As Told By His Rivals (LFCTV documentary 2024)

Liverpoolfc.com

Liverpool FC Matchday programme (2015 to 2024)

Jürgen Klopp: The Biography, Elmar Neveling (Ebury Press 2019)

Allez, Allez, Allez: The Inside Story of the Resurgence of Liverpool FC, Simon Hughes (Bantam Press 2019)

Klopp: Bring The Noise, Raphael Honigstein (Yellow Jersey Press 2019)

Robbo: Now You're Gonna Believe Us: Our Year, My Story, Andy Robertson (Reach Sport 2020)

Believe Us: How Jürgen Klopp transformed Liverpool into title winners, Melissa Reddy (Harper North 2020)

Intensity: Inside Liverpool FC, Pep Lijnders (Reach Sport 2022)

Red Men Reborn! A Social History of Liverpool Football Club from John Houlding to Jürgen Klopp, John Williams (Pitch Publishing 2022)

Jordan Henderson: The Autobiography (Michael Joseph 2022)

I Feel Fine: The Klopp 100 – A Modern Liverpool Love Affair, Chris McLoughlin & Roy Gilfoyle (Reach Sport 2022)

Sí Señor: My Liverpool Years, Roberto Firmino (Quercus 2023)